# What Others Are Saying About

## SONGS OF SAUDADES

"This poem is full of *fados*, folk songs of sorrow, of love and longing, of life and fate. It is an interwoven texture of geography, history, and personal feelings, vividly reproduc...                                   nor

                                                                            *ing*

"To return with the author to her                                          me
paths is a delight. An excellent and exciting book."

—Eleanor N. Silva, Teacher

"...a wealth of travel information...vivid descriptive imagery concerning nature and the cultural life in the Azores and Portugal."

—Bob O'Neill, Poet

"The poetry of the journey and landscape offers lovely glimpses into the everyday lives of the villagers and travelers themselves."

—Verla Flores, Author
Co-author with Dudley Gardner of
*Forgotten Frontier: A History of Wyoming Coal Mining*

"An engaging way to take the reader along this intimate family journey into the past. I feel as if I have experienced these encounters with the people and places of Portugal and the Azores. This lovely narrative poem certainly makes me want to go there."   —Ruth S. Ward, Journalist

"A wonderful gift for the arm-chair traveler...recipes are an added bonus...delightful."                —Gloria Cawthorn, Librarian

"...a free flowing of spirit recounting the memories of mind and also of heart...the staccato sounds of history."          —Helen B. Glass, Poet
Author of *Love Is Where He's At*

# SONGS OF SAUDADES

**TZEDAKAH**
PUBLICATIONS

# SONGS OF
# SAUDADES

## An Enchanting Journey
## to the Azores Islands
## and the Pousadas of Portugal

## FLORENCE INEAS NUNES

*SONGS OF SAUDADES: An Enchanting Journey to the Azores Islands and the Pousadas of Portugal.*

Copyright ©1994 by Florence Ineas Nunes.

Cover Designer: Lisa Bacchini Graphic Design and Illustration
Page Designer: Diane Nunes McCormack
Printer: Griffin Printing

**Library of Congress Cataloging-in-Publication Data**

Nunes, Florence Ineas, 1917-
    Songs of saudades: an enchanting journey to the Azores Islands
and the pousadas of Portugal / Florence Ineas Nunes.
    p.  cm.
    Includes index.
    1. Portuguese Americans—Travel—Azores—Poetry. 2. Portuguese
Americans—Travel—Portugal—Poetry. 3. Women—Travel—Portugal—
Poetry. 4. Women—Travel—Azores—Poetry. 5. Portugal—Poetry.
6. Azores—Poetry. I. Title.
PS3564.U46S6  1994    811'.54—dc20                        93—50600
                                                          CIP

ISBN: 0-929999-02-9

FIRST EDITION

10   9   8   7   6   5   4   3   2   1

*To the memory of*
*Edward Joseph Nunes*

*and to our children,*
*Edward Jr. and Diane*
*Maria and Julie*

*And to our grandchildren,*
*James and Angela.*

*They bring pleasure to my life*
*and joy to my heart.*

# CONTENTS

# FOREWORD

Journeys are always exciting experiences, whether we take them ourselves or share those of others. In this poem you will share a moving, enjoyable, and instructive adventure of a family which is exploring its roots and interrelationships. Ms. Nunes is an observant and knowledgeable traveler as well as being a sensitive poet of great skill. Persons and places really come alive under her pen. To get the best effect of her language, read the poem aloud to your family members. The experience will be most rewarding, even if you stumble on some of the foreign words—all of which are explained by the context. I heartily recommend *Songs of Saudades* to any discriminating reader of poetry.

Will C. Jumper, Ph.D.
Poet-Writer

Auburn, California

# PREFACE

**Saudades**...pronounced *Sah-u-dah´-ds*...is a word of many
meanings. The dictionary defines it as longing, yearning,
regards, and a greeting. But to me, it means much more than
the nostalgic "I love you," "I miss you," and "Goodbye until
we meet again." It is a sort of mystic, melancholy memory
tugging at the heart for what once was and fate decrees is no
more, or for what could still be, but is destined not to be.

I wrote *Songs of Saudades* to preserve for posterity our family
roots and to acquaint my family with the wealth of history in
the lands of our ancestors, Portugal and the Azores Islands. In
this endeavor, I impart to them the environmental charms of
the Islands set like a ring of gem stones in the Atlantic Ocean,
and the sense of antiquity in the legends and forests and castles
of Portugal. At the same time, I dwell on the inner emotional
soul beauty experienced in meeting another branch of our
family, coming face to face with our Atlantic cousins.

Every sentimental journey starts long before one embarks.
Something impels one to start planning an itinerary in spite of
the uncertainty of what the consequences might be. Then one
becomes aware that uncertainty spices life. When I start a
poem, I have no idea how it will evolve. The final art is always
a surprise. Although ballet dancers follow the choreography, it
is they who give the dance the gift of life by using the tools of
their talents. I am sure this holds true for composers and
performers in all the other arts, as it is in poetry. In my bringing poetry to life, I, in turn, am further enlivened by each
poem I create. And the readers bring the poem to life again
each time they read it.

# ACKNOWLEDGMENTS

My deep gratitude goes to many relatives and friends who assisted as midwives in my giving birth to *Songs of Saudades*. I begin with my Azorean ancestors who inspire curiosity, and my Atlantic cousins who were able to answer many of our questions about them and their lives.

I am grateful also to my traveling companions... my daughters Diane McCormack and Maria Egloff, my sister Clarinda Barney, and my cousin Mary Silva. They not only made my journey possible, they greatly enriched it.

I am indebted to all my relatives and friends who read the manuscripts and expressed their opinions and further encouraged me, including my colleagues who wrote endorsements for *Songs of Saudades*.

I appreciate the valuable give-and-take critiques of my fellow writers as a member of Wordsmith and Range of Light in Auburn and Chaparral and writers in the Renaissance Society in Sacramento.

I am grateful also to Tzedakah Publications and David Cawthorn, the publisher who put our book team together, including the cover artist, Lisa Bacchini. Working with them on my saudades poem has been a pleasant experience.

*Azorean Adventure*

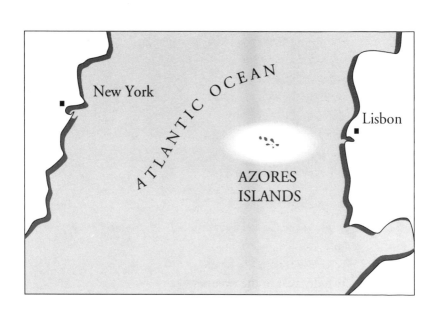

In a dreamlike daze
we are on our way
this April day to Europe
aboard United Flight 66
from Sacramento
over the Sierras.
At each ascent, I still marvel
that Man can fly.

What drama will evolve
from our journey
to explore our roots,
what will be our fate
we have no way of knowing.
The adventure begins.
There is no turning back now.
But for me, uncertainty
is one of life's best seasonings.

A forever-blue sky around us
white clouds below us
time to drift and think…
return to my childhood
to a dry year in the twenties.

Far from the Atlantic Ocean
of his Azorean Isle,
the Idaho homesteader's
boot-clad feet scatter the dust
of pulverized volcanic soil
too aware of stunted alfalfa,
dwarfed wheat heading too soon.

Question-marked forehead
sunbronzed face and sea-blue eyes,
he scans the pale, searing sky…
not a cloud in sight.
Around the Victorian farmhouse,
what is left of lawn once green
crumbles underfoot.

Like a breath of ocean breeze,
"Papa, Papa," calls
a barefoot fairylike child
flowing out the farmhouse door
rippling the ruffled skirt
of her lace-trimmed sea-blue dress.
"Do you like it?
Mama made it for my birthday."

My father was the homesteader
with the question-mark forehead.
I, the little girl
in the lace-trimmed sea-blue dress,
vowed one day years later,
after the death of my parents,
to visit the island home
of their childhood.

Sometimes I get the sensation
that the plane sits still forever
on the cloud banks, unable to move.

My mind turns the cardboard cylinder
of the kaleidoscope of my life,
my journey of geometric patterns
lit by the glow of secret yearnings
and dreams penetrating my writings
of inner journeys…

working for a living in California,
mundane tasks adorned with dreams.

Handsome Edward and I wed...
the love of my life...
wed in an October twilight.
Romance in the afterglow mingles
with the pain of adjustment
to different rhythms in each other...
living, growing,
and learning together.

We become a family,
six of us around the table...
Ed and I and Eddie,
Diane, Maria, and Julie...
again learning from each other
at work and at play,
vacations to the farm in Idaho
the seashore in Santa Cruz
camping, hiking, and goldpanning
in the Sierras...
attending theatrical musicals
and singing the songs afterwards
in our own backyard performances.
Our head of family
suffers a heart attack,
and only five of us now at the table.

An ancient wise woman
once advised,
never marry the love of your life
because when you have to part
it can be devastating.
She was right
about the devastation.

The far greater tragedy,
however,
would have been to miss
what we had together.

Artistically,
we were created for each other.
I found Ed's music
in my poetry
and he found my poetry
in his songs.
My love of the music classics
I learned from him.
He taught his daughters
to sing a mass in Latin
in three-part harmony
at very young ages.
To this day
their love of song
is a tribute to their father.
He made music fun for everyone.

Years and years
of rushed, tedious mornings
offspring to various schools
I to the office routine.
The kaleidoscope keeps turning...
I become a mother of grown children
in homes of their own
seeking their own life meanings.
I rearrange my life
sell our house
find a smaller home.

In keeping with my travel dreams,
I embark
to the first trip on my list...

a Mediterranean cruise
to Greece, Egypt, Israel
and the Greek Isles
to visit the birthplace
of Western Civilization.

The kaleidoscope revolves
to the day I inform my family
of plans to visit the next
place on my wanderer's list...
the Azores Islands
of my ancestors.
Alas, I must go alone.
My sister and my cousin decline
my travel invitations.

Surprising me a week later,
my daughters Diane and Maria phone,
"Mother, we're going with you.
But we're going to London and Paris
while you spend a week in the Azores.
Then we'll meet you in Lisbon.
The travel agency is renting a car
for us to tour
the pousadas of Portugal...
you know, antique castles
on mountaintops
restored as wayside inns
for us twentieth-century travelers."
"I get it," I say, reviving.
"Then we three return to the Azores
to finish our stay."

At an after-Christmas dinner,
we sit around the table
discussing our April journey.
I ask Cousin Mary,

"Doesn't it sound like fun?"
"Yes," she replies,
"Is it too late to join you?"
We assure her there is yet time,
suggest she call the travel agency.

A week later my sister
Clarinda phones from Idaho,
in a rather weak voice, asks,
"Is it too late to join you?"
"Wonderful," I say,
"but what changed your mind?"
"My family ganged up on me,
said this might be my last chance
to visit the Azores
unless I want to go alone."
I rejoice as she continues.
 "I even said I couldn't afford it.
They said what you always say,
'Sell one of your Arabian horses.'"

She asks about the plane.
"You sound afraid."
She admits fright,
fear of flying over water.
I reason with her
that most people die in bed
yet she goes to bed every night
and nothing happens.

The next day I phone the agency
and my travel folder bulges
to include the five of us.

Portraits for passports
hurry, hurry, hurry...
frantic letters fortnightly

back and forth to the Azores…
the mail is much too slow.
We shop, prepare homes to be left,
learning, reading, researching,
travel agency conferences…
friends apprised of plans
giving bon-voyage parties.

A before-the-journey Easter party
in my Sierra hilltop home
in California.
Lilacs and poppies bloom beside
trees with tiny green almonds,
trees laden with marble-size fruit.
Wild deep-pink roses bloom
along the terraces.

At the airport
Diane embraces husband Frank,
son Jim and daughter Angela,
the teenagers clinging to her.
One last kiss for Maria and Tom.
In a flurry of goodbyes, we leave
for the waiting terminal.
As we sit waiting for the plane,
we hear Diane paged.
She answers the nearest phone.
"Mom," says Jim,
"I just wanted to hear your voice
once more."

We enter the plane,
unconsciously
establishing a pattern
for the entire journey.
Maria boards first,
hoping for an empty seat beside her

for her movie camera
and the VCR on wheels.
Diane follows to help her.
Quick-moving Clarinda follows them.
Mary, moving much more slowly,
finally negotiates the stairs.
I bring up the rear,
determined to see
everyone into the plane
before I step inside.

The kaleidoscope stops turning.
The plane flies over white clouds
above the Rocky Mountains
past the prairie states
over the industrial East
from Pacific to Mountain to Central
to Eastern time.

We arrive at Kennedy Airport
in the dwindling hours of afternoon
to board the planes to Europe...
Diane and Maria on United to London;
Clarinda, Mary, and I on TAP,
Transport Air Portugal,
to the Island of Terceira.
We embrace my daughters,
parting and reviewing plans to meet
the following week in Lisbon.

Our party dwindled to three,
an empty feeling in my stomach,
my sister and my cousin and I
wander aimlessly till nightfall
around drabby, not-too-clean walls,
shabby rugs and formica chairs.
We check in at the TAP counter,

walk to the new red-carpeted corridor
to the TAP waiting area,
to inviting overstuffed chairs
lamps and end tables to await
the night plane to Terceira.
This is our introduction
to a Portuguese-speaking environment.

Strapped to plush blue velvet chairs
aboard the plane we watch
New York Harbor lights disappear.

Attendants hand us baroque menus...

> *Oferta de Vinhos de Mesa Portugueses*
>     Wine from the Portuguese Table
> *Salada de Estacão*
>     Salad in Season
> *Medalhos de Lombo de Vaca*
>     Rib Roast of Beef
> *Couve-Flor "Polonaise"*
>     Polish Colewort (cabbage)
> *Arroz a Espanhola*
>     Spanish Rice
> *ou Lombo de Porco a Trensmontana*
>     or Rib Roast of Pork
> *Feijae Verde-Batata Assadas*
>     Green Beans-Baked Potatoes
> *Queijo-Crackers*
>     Cheese-Crackers
> *Pastelaria Francesca*
>     French Pasteries
> *Cafe e Cha*
>     Coffee and Tea

We dine. We read. We doze,
resting our heads on white pillows,
woolen plaid coverlets over us,

lights turned low through the night,
only darkness outside the windows.

I turn on my light
to scan a hodge-podge
of information
assembled from our travel guides
and many travel agency brochures
plus stories I remember
hearing my parents relate.

The Azores Islands...
a string of nine jewels
in the North Atlantic
two-thirds of the way
straight as the birds fly
from New York to Portugal
named AÇORES
for numerous eagle-hawk birds
once swarming the archipelago.

Corvo, Flores, Graciosa,
Santa Maria, Pico, São Jorge,
Faial, Terceira, São Miguel...
scarred by volcanos and molten lavas
warmed by the gulf stream...
wrapped in green
incense trees, ferns, vines,
camellias, azalias, hibiscus,
oleander, loquats, oranges, lemons,
figs, tea plants, daisies,
hydrangeas, and the elephant ears
of taro root...all grow at sea level
and up the mountainsides...
at high altitudes, hardy evergreen
junipers and sequoia.

Mysterious mountaintops,
some say,
of legendary Atlantis…
dominated by mighty, mystic Pico
rising seven thousand feet
above the sea,
forever forming circles
of white smoke,
its summit in the clouds.

The Islands became bases
in the 1400s for adventures
in unknown waters
in the North Atlantic all the way
to Labrador and Greenland.

Colonized in the 1500s…
Portuguese seafarers and whalers,
descendants of invading Moors,

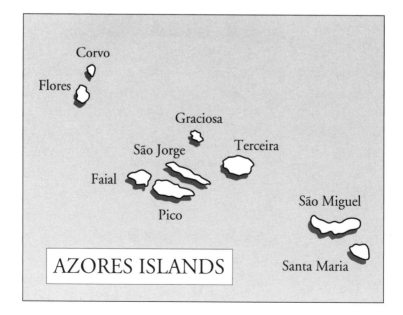

Corvo

Flores

Graciosa

São Jorge

Terceira

Faial

Pico

São Miguel

AZORES ISLANDS

Santa Maria

later merchants from Italy
and Flemish refugees of war.
Corn-grinding windmills
and adapted architecture
identify their lands of origin.

Invaded by Hispania,
later driven out by force…
pillaged by coastal pirates,
the Islands are linked by location
to historical western events.
American, French, British,
and NATO airbases continue
the archipelago's role
in the saga of Earth's history.

Emerging pre-dawn light
and the slowly descending plane
awaken me to peer below.
A light flickering here and there,
shapes of pinpoint islands appear
in the vast Atlantic space.
Wrapped in the ray
of the rising sun,
we land on the Island of Terceira,
land in the middle of a concrete strip.
Uniformed air attendants
roll a set of metal stairs
for our descent from the plane.
Clutching our carry-on luggage
we walk to the *aeroporto*.

After going through customs,
our baggage in wire carts,
we settle for a four-hour wait,
breakfast on hard rolls and cheese,
body rhythms disoriented

in a new time zone…
catnap the hours away
until time to board
a small island passenger plane
with the Rolls-Royce symbol
that gives us our first glimpse
of the Volcano Pico,
its peak reveling in the sunshine,
mist obliterating its base,
a mystic cone suspended in the sky.

We land at the *aeroporto* at Horta
bordered with multicolored flowers
in the Island of Faial,
hop a taxi for a six-mile drive
to the inter-island launch.

Promptly at noon
the launch arrives.
Luggage is loaded in the hold
followed by wicker baskets
filled with produce and baked goods
covered with embroidered cloths.
The boat, a large white gliding swan,
rolls in rhythm
with the swelling Atlantic waves.

Wordless, in the Portuguese chatter,
we flow along in a symphony of water
sky and April sunshine.
Assembled on the shores of Pico Island,
a multitude of cousins awaits us.
We meet for the first time
in embraces, smiles, misty eyes,
forced to speak our limited word
knowledge of our ancestral tongue.

We drive through Madalena
along the ocean roadway
to the Village of Santo Amaro.
Too early for spring greenery,
the eye picks up terraced plots
fenced in black volcanic rock
ebony stone houses, some stuccoed
in designs of black and white.
Overwhelmed with jet lag
we doze momentarily
with smells of the surrounding sea
sounds of waves washing sand
in a world of black and white
broken by pink profusions
of azaleas growing wild
on roadsides and the hillsides…
we awake to comment politely
only to doze again.

The car stops and jerks us awake
at Cousin Gloria's house
wherein dwell daughter Fatima,
son-in-law Amaro Soares Melo,
granddaughters Marilia and Mara.

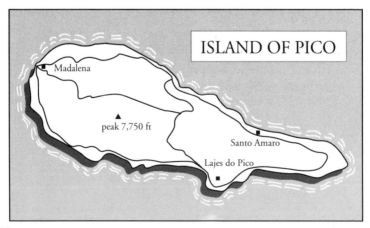

Aware of our need for sleep
and our waning appetites for lunch,
our cousins send us to our rooms,
insisting we sleep away our weariness.

In late afternoon
we awake refreshed
in a strange house
in a strange land
among strange surroundings…
we have yet to orient ourselves.

Together with our cousins
we walk from the waterfront
to a recreation home, an *adega*,
in the hills of Terra Alta
where my mother was born,
sip Angelica
in the basement wineroom,
walk down the hills
to the rock-strewn shore.

Clarinda complains
she can't remember Portuguese words
she spoke as a child.
"Don't worry," I say,
"soon you will recall what you knew
dredged from your subconscious."
In the meantime, I remember
to interpret for her.

Seated on and leaning against
black sun-warmed boulders,
we watch the sun go down,
walk back up the hills
in the rosy afterglow
to dine by candlelight.

Fish in
Uncooked Sauce

*Peixe em
Molho Cru*

page 156

Fish served in a succulent sauce,
linguica sausage and taro root,
greens and potatoes, red dinner wine,
homemade breads with butter,
caramel flan and cupcakes.
By evening's end
a fascinating warmth seeps around
our get-acquainted conversations
with our Atlantic cousins.

Sunday mass
at the Church of Santo Amaro
offered for our departed ancestors…
a black-and-white stone and stucco
structure,
1736 etched above the portal,
white walls inside and beamed ceilings…
statues of Santo Amaro, Santa Ana,
Nosa Senhora de Carmo,
carved in colored stone
motifs of aquamarine and gold baroque…
music and gospel in Portuguese,
greetings of well-wishing cousins.

One morning we awaken to the sound
of pelting, wind-driven rain.
The North Atlantic wind violently
whips waves, thrashing the shore
relentlessly.
Now we understand the sea-power
that had knocked out
one end of the two-foot-wide
six-foot-high solid concrete wall
erected fify yards inland
along the length of the village
to keep the sea

from the coastal stone dwellings
like the one housing our cousins.

We shiver in the cold house and
everything in it seems damp.
Towards morning we hear Mary.
"Are you cold, too?" she asks,
standing at our door.
"Do you want to get in bed with us?"
I ask. She nods.
I move closer to Clarinda
and we three snuggle
to warm each other. Mary says,
"I always wanted a sister."

Amaro checks on the cattle
grazing up in the mountains,
reports snow falling on the *serras*,
snow that usually falls only
on the tip of Pico.
After the two-day Atlantic storm,
just as if nothing has happened,
the sun returns to warm us.

Although thoroughly immersed
in Portuguese customs and speech,
never have I felt more American.
We are introduced as
"our American cousins,"
referred to as the *Americanas*
in friendly tones of esteem.

Many villagers remember Mary.
In the late 1940s
she and her brother,
accompanied by their mother,

whom we called Tia Lucinda,
visited in Santo Amaro.

"My mother had vowed as she prayed,"
said Mary, "that if my brother
came home alive from World War II,
she would sponsor
a Holy Spirit Festival
for the entire village.
Frank came home alive and well
and Mother kept her vow."
I remember hearing
that the plane had faltered
right after takeoff.
The pilot returned them safely.
Tia Lucinda courageously boarded
a second plane to keep her promise.

In good weather
Gloria and Fatima arrange rinsed
dishes on the graveled portion
of the courtyard
to dry in the sun.
In the kitchen, modern appliances
stand side by side
with a built-in ancient oven
that baked unleavened bread, *bolo*,
for our ancestors of the 1500s.
Gloria still bakes *bolo*
in the coals of the oven
for special *festas*
along with round loaves
of crusty wheat bread.

Across the courtyard,
next to a large storeroom,
two chiseled tubs

Unleavened
Cake-Bread

*Bolo do Forno*

*page 151*

made from large lava boulders,
one carved in front as a washboard,
occupy a small room
for use in summer droughts
when the automatic washer
cannot operate.
Alongside deep underground,
an old cistern collects rainwater.
A pail, with a rope fastened to it,
draws water for the rock tubs,
one for washing and one for rinsing.

We enter the house
from the courtyard
to a hallway
between the kitchen and dining room.
A large table dominates the area,
serving as both dining room
and living room, a couch
and chair at one end,
leading to a hallway
that serves four bedrooms and a bath…
all situated over a basement room
for sewing and other tasks.

Stairs down from the courtyard
lead straight to the street,
turning left to the village,
or right to Terra Alta
or enclosed upstairs to a balcony
adjacent to the far bedroom
above the street and seawall
where we watch the ocean
restlessly ebbing and flowing
forever chiseling
jagged rocks into rounded boulders
warmed by the sun…

look north
to the Ilha de São Jorge
and the never-ending Atlantic
blending with the sky,
almost obliterating the horizon.

Clarinda talks with Amaro,
compares Azorean and Idaho
farming in the same volcanic soil.
The difference lies in the weather,
seabreezes and moisture in one
and dry desert summers with winter
snow in the other.
She marvels that nature provides
all the necessary rainwater in the island,
while irrigation water collected
in reservoirs in the spring runoff
becomes the lifeblood
of farming in Idaho.

Amaro shows her the various
plants and legumes
in the lava enclosures
designed for their one milk cow
and the beef cattle, providing
in sequence the necessary protein,
no chemical fertilizers, but
a system of recycling wastes
as in the farm in Idaho.
Other enclosures behind the storeroom
on the other side of the courtyard
contain chickens for eggs
and a couple of pigs for food later on.
Various plots enclose gardens
of vegetables for the table,
others grapevines and fruit trees.

In a morning walk to the *adega*
Amaro points out
the built-in grape press
occupying a corner.
Large barrels on their sides
hold red lunch and dinner wine.
One nearby holds the Angelica,
a sweet dessert wine.
We drink from tiny pottery cups,
feeling its warmth within us,
warmth to match
the hospitality we enjoy.

Gloria relates to us her memories
of stories told
by the grandmother we share...
about the courtship of Mariana,
Clarinda's and my mother.
We tell her of our father, Antonio,
having arrived in Sacramento
as a young man.
No money to buy land,
he headed north to Idaho
to homestead.

After clearing the land
of sagebrush and lava rocks
to establish a farm,
American Anthony, nicknamed Tony,
built a white Victorian house
and gained title to the land.

Tony visited Santo Amaro
to see about finding a wife
and to console his father
and come to terms
with the death of his mother.

A cousin mentioned our grandfather,
who had three single daughters,
the oldest already married.
They called one day.
Mariana sat by a window
embroidering a pillowcase.
Her sisters sat around
occupied with genteel tasks
still dressed in their Sunday best,
having already attended mass.

Antonio approached Mariana,
"Have you ever thought
of going to America?"
"Yes. I have, but I know
I'll never be that fortunate."

After a few visits,
the truth became apparent to everyone.
Antonio preferred Mariana
and started his courtship.
The two walked hand-in-hand
along the street we now walk
in front of Gloria's house.

Sometimes Antonio brought with him
his little motherless sister,
eight-year-old Amelia.
Mariana and her sisters adored her,
but she preferred our grandmother,
the mother figure.

Antonio and Mariana married,
made the long ship and railroad
journey to Idaho,
accompanied by his father
and his little sister.

I remember Mother telling
of a submarine scare
they experienced on the voyage
during the war year of 1915.


When I was just a toddler
and Clarinda an infant,
our father died
from undrained liquid in the lungs
in the aftermath
of World War I influenza.


Complaining cries of night birds
trouble us at first.
"Those are seabirds
forced ashore at night by nature.
They cry because they cannot
stand to be separated
from the freedom of the sea,"
Amaro tells us.


As Gloria and I stroll
the hillside streets of the village,
she introduces me
as Mariana's daughter
to a tall elderly man with a cane.
He remembers my mother.
"But what of Clarinda?" he asks,
Clarinda, my mother's younger sister
for whom my sister is named.
Gloria reminds him
of Aunt Clarinda's death.
"Tall and slender,
the most beautiful face in the village,"
he reminisces.
"She glowed like a star in the heavens."

Our first dinner invitation
comes from Gloria's brother,
Cousin Silverio Teixeira Gomes
and his wife Maria,
held at the home
of their newly married daughter
Arminda, and husband Helio Simas.
To our delight,
Arminda speaks a little English.
Their home is a restored
old lava-rock house
on the hill
across from Amaro's *adega*.
Helio painstakingly roasts fish
on an outdoor grill.
We manage rapid, entertaining
Portuguese conversation.

Another evening we dine
at Silverio's and Maria's,
now owners of my mother's house.
We listen to a program
of poets reading on television
classic and modern poetry.
I picture my mother
and my aunts as girls
growing up in these very rooms,
reading many of the same verses.

I marvel that poetry,
a vital part of my life,
I happily encounter
wherever I go.

Cousins on my father's side
invite us to dinner,
Jose Lourenco Nunes Vargas

and his wife Aurea,
daughter Maria Luis,
sons Manuel and Rubene.
They live on a hillside
in the village a mile away.
Jose Lourenco's mother,
Maria do Carmo Nunes,
gives me important details
to add to our family history.
She tells me how we are related.
My husband was her cousin
on the Nunes side.
Her husband was my cousin
on the Inacio side.

We attend a noontime dinner party
at the home of Mary's cousin
Maria Helena and husband
Jose Leonardo Gomes Goulart
and little daughter Monica.
Also invited are her brothers
Felipe Teixeira da Silva
and wife Maria Izilda,
Manuel Inacio Melo da Silva
and wife Estela Maria.
They all speak English, but much
prefer their native tongue.
After dinner, we sing along
with Jose and his viola.
I miss Diane and Maria
and their distinctive alto voices.

Everyone assembles for photographs,
strolls to Manuel's *adega* nearby
for a taste of his Angelica.

Maria Izilda and Filipe
invite us to lunch at their home
on the other side of the Island.
We tour their new hotel
soon to open in Cais do Pico,
much needed for foreign visitors
with no close island relatives.
Maria plans to serve motel guests
typical Azorean fare.
Links of linguiça sausage
hang above the kitchen range
near shelves of herbs and spices.
In a polished massive cabinet
we see jugs of red Pico wine
and bottles of homemade Angelica.

We meet their teenagers
Luis and Elizabeth,
arriving home after school,
loaded with books and papers.

Azorean children
walking to and from school
with their books and lunch boxes
look very much the same
as our American school children.
They prize denim jeans and sneakers.

We tour the Island
capturing landscapes in cameras,
walking alongside the Atlantic,
watching the waves break
in the various moods of the sea,
talking with friendly villagers,
hearing the anecdotes about relatives
long gone from Earth...
lunches here, dinners there,

walks to *adega* winerooms
to sip Angelica…
the week melts into the sea,
merges with the briny air.

Aboard the launch in early morning,
we three leave the Island of Pico.
The volcano, its dome swathed in snow,
stands statuelike in the mist.
Borne on the swells of the Atlantic
we speed by two ancient cliffs
rising out of the sea…
mountaintops of Atlantis?
Still low on the horizon, the sun
flashes the tips of undulating waves.

I wander back across the years,
reciting again with my third-grade class,
"Behind him lay the grey Azores
Beyond the Gates of Hercules.
Before him not the ghost of shores.
Before him only shoreless seas."
Like the Gates of Hercules, the two
seacliffs guard the entrance to Pico.
Lulled completely in sea rhythm, the
approaching shore of Faial startles me.
The Island of Pico has disappeared
in the morning mist.

We have a day's wait.
Our plane will come in late afternoon,
time to tour the Island of Faial by taxi.

Faial, a lacing of volcanic rock
dubbed the Blue Island…
hydrangas
grow in rows shaped into fences

surrounding agricultural plots,
blooming blue in the summer months.

We drive by new mammoth hills
ascended from the sea
in volcanic eruptions of the 1950s,
green appearing in the crevices.
In the give and take
of volcanic violence,
other mountains disappeared
into the surrounding seas.

We drive around the remains
of ancient Capelinhos Volcanos,
the Caldeira Crater, a place
of silence carpeted in green,
past Horta Harbor with yachts of all
nations, rejoice that one yacht
flies our star-spangled banner.

The taxi leaves us at the *aeroporto*.
We check our luggage,
lunch leisurely,
while away the hours…
walk beside flower borders
of pink azaleas, daisies
and other unknown flowers,
venture into neighborhoods
of white houses and red tile roofs,
converse as we rest and read
or just meditate and think.

I turn on a fountain
and no water gushes out.
The woman at the counter
tells us the water line is broken.
It will take a while to fix it.

She suggests bottled soft drinks
or that we ask for water
at one of the houses across the street.
Seeing the look on our faces
she assures us it is acceptable.
My intense dislike of
the sweetness of soft drinks
drives me to knock at a door.
A young woman answers.
I ask for a glass of water,
explaining that the water line
at the *aeroporto* has broken.
She smiles and goes to fetch it,
appears with three glasses.

I pour the water into my canteen.
We all say, "*Obrigado.*"
I offer her
the ever-popular American dollar.
She declines,
saying she is happy to oblige us.
I say something about hoping
to return the favor someday.
She suggests that I return it
to another person somewhere
in an ongoing
international chain of favors.

Half an hour before takeoff
a group of ball players
in white-and-blue uniforms
exuding youthful exuberance
thunder in and fill the area
followed by a tired-looking
middle-aged man.
"He must be the coach," I say.
Their conversation reveals

they are playing soccer
with a rival school
in Ponta Delgada.
They board the plane before us.

The intercom announces
as we leave the *aeroporto* at Horta,
"The pilot will encircle the volcano
so you can see Pico covered with snow
from last week's Atlantic storm."
We look down on the piercing peak,
its crystal crags reflecting the sun,
its lower half still hidden in the mist.

Ed would have loved the sight,
would have captured it in his camera…
would have loved Pico Island
much as he loved Sausalito,
the town of his youth,
in California.

"*Adeus*, Goodbye,
my Island, my ancestors,
until we return again
two weeks from today,"
I call out in silence
as we ascend far above the waves
on our way
to the Island of São Miguel
to board TAP Flight 198Y to Lisbon.

*Pousadas of Portugal*

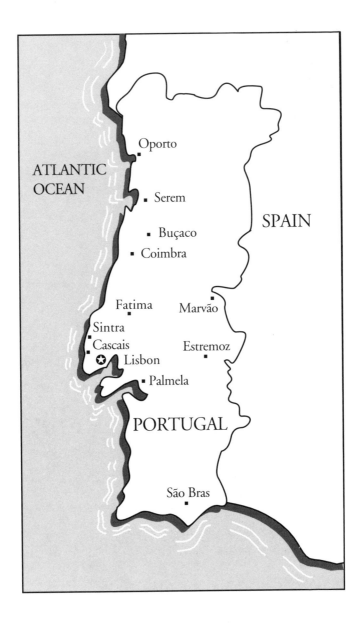

 We land in Portugal
after midnight.
I look in vain for my daughters.
Diane waves from the other side
of a glass wall.
Thank God, they are here.

"Mother, have you any *escudos?*"
asks Maria, embracing me.
"I need them to get our rental car
out of the parking lot."
I hand her six thousand *escudos,*
worth about six American dollars.

We find our luggage in a turmoil
of wire carts and people
and fill our car trunk
up to behind our heads
in the burgundy subcompact.
We drive to Cascais,
studying maps and streets
deserted after midnight.
We pass Estoril in the Atlantic's
southwestern corner
of the European Continent...
arrive at the Citadel Hotel
at three in the morning to begin
our two-week visit in Portugal.

Diane and I enter the office.
I confirm our reservations,
conversing in Portuguese.

The man in charge expresses delight
that I speak his native tongue.

"Mom, how great,"
says Diane, afterwards.
"You can speak the language.
That's what we missed in Paris.
I suppose they were insulted
that we could not speak French.
That could account
for their rude indifference to us.
At least, they came across that way."

After a late breakfast
that will serve as lunch, also,
we explore Cascais
our home for two days…
time to catch up on my journal,
time to sum up our visit
in Santo Amaro, and to acquaint
Diane and Maria with a preview
of Our Island.

Cascais
an old fishing village
attracted artists and writers
in the 1930s.
Modernized now,
only fishermen and the sea remain.

We drive to a very old castle
on a hillside
with shops and a park nearby.
Maria lugs her camera.
Diane carries the attached VCR
over cobbled walkways.
Maria films a man and a woman

sitting on a bench in the park.
They express delight
when she shows them
their tiny pictures
as she reels the tape.

Coming down the many stairs
we had climbed to the turret,
Diane laughs as she says,
"I have this irresistible impulse
to hurl the VCR down the stairs
and be free of the burden."

After dining in the hotel,
we assemble in our room,
settle down in our night clothes.
I read to my companions
some of the history of Portugal
I had compiled.

Portugal
in the Iberian Peninsula
land of the first European seafarers,
already communicated with Britain,
Ireland, and European seaports
at the end of the Neolithic Age,
a prelude to Portuguese expansion.

Lusitanians,
dwelling between
the River Tejo and the River Douro,
led by Chief Variathus,
built an agricultural system
and a network of townships and roads.

For two centuries
the Romans fought

freedom-loving Lusitanians.
King Augustus, from 27 B.C.
to 24 A.D., drove out Roman invaders.
Northern Lusitania and Galicia
formed the Kingdom of Suevi.

After the collapse of Rome
in the fifth century,
Germanic invaders established
the Visigothic Monarchy.
Invaders, assimilated into Romanism,
abandoned Arianism.

Invasion by the Arabs in 711
ended the Monarchy of Visigoths.
Hispanogoths took refuge
in the Asturian Mountains,
later founded Christian monarchies,
drove out Arab invaders,
liberating their descendants,
the Mozoarabs.

Terra Portuguesa
in the 11th Century
became a province
distinct from Galicia,
self-governing master of its destiny...
bounded northerly by Galicia
bounded southerly by the Arabs,
given to Henry of Burgundy in 1095,
son-in-law of Alfonso VI
of Castile and Leon.
The Dynasty of Burgundy began.

Portuguese language
of Latin origin emerged,
enriched with German,

Gaelic and Arabian,
with a sprinkle of Oriental words...
diplomatic language of travelers
from the 15th to 18th Centuries
to Far East via Cape of Good Hope...
spoken in Azores Islands and Madeira,
Cape Verde, Guinea, São Tome Islands,
Angola and Mozambique,
Portuguese India, Macao,
Timor and Brazil.

Literature emerged
in the 11th Century,
collections of verses,
*cantigas coita* expressed
sufferings of maidens in love.
King Denis, a poet,
founded University of Coimbra
in the 1020s.
Grandson Dom Pedro and Mistress
Ines de Castro influenced art
and literature and courtly living.

Counselors of Pedro's father,
Alfonso IV, persuaded the king
for the sake of the dynasty
to behead the lovely Ines.
When Pedro I ascended the throne
he granted posthumously
queenship to his beloved Ines.

Successors to the throne in dispute,
John, natural son of Pedro I,
ascended the throne as John I,
founder of the Avis Dynasty.

Most brilliant period of expansion
in Portuguese history
began in 1415...
conquest of Ceuta and Morocco
by son of John I.
Prince Henrique the Navigator
and his expert mariners
in navigation,
cosmology and cartography,
sailed lengthy voyages
to the Atlantic Isles
off the Coast of Africa,
established trading centers,
colonized the desert isles.

In 1494
the world was divided
by the reigning pope
between Portugal and Spain.

Vasco Nunes de Gama went to India,
Pedro Alvaras Cabral to Brazil.
Fernando de Magellan crossed
the uncharted Pacific Ocean
in a voyage around the world.

Portugal controlled a vast empire
from Morocco to East Indies
and Territory of Brazil
via trading stations
and coastal towns,
with no subjugation
of native peoples.
Conqueror Alfonso de Albuquerque
conquered Goa, Malacca, Hormuz,
and a bit of India.

Lack of following colonizers,
dissension among leaders,
distance, greed and rivalry
of other emerging nation powers
began the eventual disintegration
of the Portuguese Empire,
an empire that paved the way
for the spread
of European civilization
and the spread of Christianity…
brought to Europe new plants,
sugar, tea, spices, tobacco,
made of Lisbon a bazaar
of gold and precious stones
and Oriental spices.

King John III
abandoned some conquered cities.
King Sebastian, youthful visionary
desiring Christianity for Morocco,
was killed in Quivir in 1558
in the Battle of Alcazar,
ending the last Portuguese Dynasty,
the Avis Dynasty.

Portugal's sixty years
of Spanish captivity
ended in 1640.

The earthquake of 1755 destroyed
most of the City of Lisbon.

Because of alliance with England
since 1386,
Portugal never submitted completely
to the blockade
imposed by Napoleon.

Portugal lost most of its empire,
retaining Goa,
Angola and Mozambique.
Brazil proclaimed independence
in 1822.
Political struggles, revolutions,
civil war…Berlin Conference
fixed limits of African Colonies.

King Carlos I
and Crown Prince Luis
were assassinated in 1908.
After a two-year reign of Manuel II,
Portugal proclaimed itself a Republic…
sent troops to France
in World War I
as an ally of Britain.

Salazar began in 1926
forty-two years of dictatorship.

Portugal remained neutral
in World War II,
yet collaborated with Atlantic Policy
in defense of the West.

The forty-two years
of Portuguese dictatorship
ended with Salazar's death
in 1968.

Portuguese Independence Day
April 25, 1974…
Dictator Caetano and President Thomaz
were exiled to Brazil.

Years of war
with Angola and Mozambique,
economic chaos,
U.N. censure.
Azores and Madeira
threatened secession.
Independence finally was granted
in 1975 to Cape Verde,
Angola and Mozambique.

Portugal joined
the European Economy
January 1, 1986.

Country of great lyricists
dreaming of past glories,
immortalized in "Os Lusiadas"
by Poet Luis de Camões...
this is the country we tour
in the springtime...
Portugal in April.

We drive to the Sintra
of marble quarries,
detour around the City
to accommodate
the international car races,
pass green miles of countryside
to the royal palace at Queluz,
a replica
of the Palace of Versailles
with its Hall of Mirrors...
dine in the 18th-Century kitchen,
Cozinha Velha,
once the kitchen of the palace,
sip a special white wine,
enjoy poached sea bass,

grilled pork on a spit,
apples and cheese,
vanilla souffle.

Waterlilies float in fountain ponds
of blue *azulejos*
in antique courtyards.
Florentine marble
as used by Michelangelo,
Iberian and Flemish tapestries,
indigo blue ceramics,
carpets from Rabat,
porcelain from Austria,
and Portuguese Chippendale
adorn the palace rooms.
The palace of today's state banquets,
was the birthplace of Pedro I.
Our visiting President Eisenhower
once was housed in its royal chambers.

We drive through Mafra,
through Ericeira back to Cascais
to start our tour the next day
of the *pousadas*,
those old castles restored as inns
of tranquility, offering
rest for us weary travelers.

Ericeira and Mafra again
sixty miles
through a valley of vineyards,
white houses, rolling countrysides...
windmills of round white bases with
blue stripes painted at ground level,
peaked roofs
each with a mast and four sails
stretched by ropes...

cobblestone streets
hundreds of years old,
golden towers and ramparts in the rain
up a hill to the Castle of Obidos,
given by Poet King Dinis
to his Queen Isabella,
to the Estalagem do Convento,
an old village nunnery.

This is our introduction
to *pousada* lodging.
Our reservations include two rooms
furnished with two single beds,
a room for Diane and Maria,
a room for Clarinda, Mary, and me.
Because I am the fortunate one
who possesses a healthy back,
I sleep on the cot.

Along with airline tickets,
we also paid for lodging
and continental breakfasts
of sweet rolls and coffee.
Whatever else we order
is charged to our rooms,
including dinners.
To make paying more simple,
each one takes her turn
paying the *pousada* charges
when we check out,
except for phone calls
paid by the callers.

We lunch in our rooms,
rooms with four-poster beds
canopied in rich brocades,
one set red, one set green,

Sweet Bread

*Pão Doce*

*page 153*

eat Espírito Santo bread with cheese
our Azorean cousins packed for us,
and strawberries, apples and oranges
from a market in Estoril.

We stroll in the soft rain
protected by umbrellas
through ancient convent grounds,
mingling gnarled tangerine
trees, grapevines, roses in bloom,
bring home an opening red bud
and place it in a glass of water
on a window sill.

Mr. Garcia,
owner of the pub,
a converted wine cellar,
talks with us of our respective
countries, of American television…
"O Barque de Amor,"
translated as "The Love Boat,"
and "Dallas," pronounced "Dahlus."
We watch an American TV film
with Portuguese captions
as we sip their famous port wine.
Upstairs we dine
in a spacious room
with heavy black beams.
A fire burns
in a massive corner fireplace
made of native stone.

We three always awaken early,
shower and dress,
head for the dining room
to breakfast.
We return to pack,

wondering if the girls have awakened.
"One of you knock on their door
or phone them," I suggest,
"because if I do,
they will be angry with me."
So Mary and Clarinda take turns.

Past our car windows
fly the town signs…
Caldas da Rainha,
São Martinho do Porto,
Alcobaça, Nazare, Batalha,
Leiria, on the way
to the 1800-foot climb
through the mountains
to the Forest of Buçaco.

Eucalyptus and pink-and-blue
clustered hydrangeas intermingle
with various shades of green
vines, ferns, pines and cork trees,
stately cedars and crooked cypresses.
Bubbly cool water flows
from natural mountain springs
on forest battlegrounds
where the British Wellington
defeated the Napoleonic legions,
thwarted an invasion of Iberia,
then slept away his weariness
in one of the cloister cells.

We reach the Palace of Buçaco
and the royal hunting lodge,
built from a partly torn-down
monastery of 1628,
walled for isolation
of barefoot Carmelites.

The Palace was the favorite dwelling
of King Carlos and Queen Amelia.
The queen lived in exile in England
since 1910, after the assassination
of King Carlos and Crown Prince Luis
and the advent of the Republic.

The Palace was erected
high on a mountain
in the center of the forest.
From our second-floor rooms,
we walk the grand staircase.
Ornate marble balustrade
and blue tile frescoes
line the staircase walls.

Maria, camera in hand,
charms a guard for permission
to climb the tower
to film the countryside.
He obliges and leads the way
up spiraling stairs.
No interpretation is necessary
as we behold the forest
from on high.
He can read the exclamation points
in our eyes.

I well relate to the myth
about the *saudades* God felt
for the lost Eden
that inspired Him
to create another Eden,
the Forest of Buçaco.

We dress for dinner,
Clarinda in a red dress

and black leather boots,
Mary in a white creation
trimmed in blue,
I in a white-topped
print-skirted dirndl gown,
Maria in a white dress
trimmed in pastel colors,
and Diane in her favorite colors,
burgundy and teal.
We enter the theatrical splendor
in the dining room,
sip ruby-red and lemon-colored
*dao* wine of the region,
dine at tables set
with ornate crystal and silver,
bouquets of azaleas,
gaze at Gothic wooden ceilings.
Through two huge arched-wall windows,
we view the lit-up terrace
and perfectly trimmed gardens
sloping to the dark forest
around the Palace.

Between courses,
I ask my daughters,
"Remembering our distant struggles
in your growing-up years,
would you have believed it
if a fortune teller in the 1960s
as she looked in her crystal ball
had seen us now elegantly dressed
dining at the Palace of Buçaco?"

After breakfast we wend our way
through the same pathways
we had strolled to see the sunset...
cobblestone stairs

up and down the hills
passing wayside fountains
shrines and chapels
moss-covered pathways
benches by vine-covered tree trunks.

Birds sing and sunlight flashes
jewels through trees and shrubs
and tangled vines
in this enchanted forest.
Like *Brigadoon,*
I feel that as soon as we leave
the forest will disappear forever.

At noon we leave the castle,
wander in the car
through other parts of the forest
stop at the Cruz Alta,
the high cross,
climb the stairs to the top
for a last look
north and south
east and west
at the Forest of Buçaco.

Like the exiled Queen Amelia
when she left
after being permitted a visit in 1945,
I silently say,
"Goodbye forever."

We drive past
Sangalhos and Anadia...
the brochures say
are villages of sparkling wines...
the spas of Curia and Luso,
beaches of Mira,

Buarcos and Figueira da Foz,
we come to Serem
and the Pousada de Santo Antonio
high on a mountain.

The red brick floor at the entrance
is wet with glossy varnish.
So we enter via the kitchen.
Cooking aromas tempt our hunger.
After checking into
second-floor rooms,
we return for a lentil soup version
of *caldo verde* for lunch.

Green Soup

*Caldo Verde*

*page 155*

We drive to a winery at Porto
where port wine is shipped
to English drawing rooms.
Mad traffic and the rebuilding
of the highway through town
cause our too-late arrival
after closing hours.
We enjoy an almost traffic-free
drive back to the pousada,
leisurely partake of a trout dinner.

"Tell us more about the Azores,"
says Maria as she finishes dessert
and stirs her coffee.

Clarinda voices amazement again
that their windmills
are not used for pumping water
but for grinding grains into flour.
Rain provides all the water for crops
grown in small plots,
enclosed in fences
of black volcanic rocks,

rocks that had to be cleared
before the soil could be tilled.

The rocks absorb the day's sun
to warm growing vegetables,
grass, vines, and fruit trees,
offering protection
from the cold Atlantic night wind.

"They grow the perfect protein,"
Clarinda explains,
"for their dairy cows
by planting certain legumes,
plants and grasses,
and orderly rotate the cattle
from one enclosure to another.
The beef cattle graze in the
mountains and drink from the
many lakes they call *lagos*.
Imagine how easy farming
would be in Idaho if summer
irrigation was not necessary."

A woman sitting with her husband
at the next table
speaks of her interest
in Azorean farming,
after overhearing Clarinda's account.
The couple relate their challenges
and ways of dry farming
in their ranch in Canada.

A walk in the garden
by starlight inspires us
to gather strength in restful sleep
to tour Coimbra tomorrow.

Coimbra
the most romantic of old cities
inspired the song,
"April In Portugal,"
it is said.

Up narrow winding cobble streets
we go, fearing we can go no farther
and yet cannot turn around,
round and round to the top
to the university,
second oldest in the world...
founded in Lisbon in the 1020s,
entrenched in Coimbra in 1537,
whence came, among others,
Poet Luis de Camões...
17th-Century portal, Via Latina,
Sala de Capelos
for graduating ceremonies,
portrait gallery of kings,
University Chapel
with 16th-Century organ,
16th-Century candelabra,
17th-Century tiles...
baroque university library
with a million volumes,
tables of ebony and rosewood
imported from India and Brazil,
jade and lemon marble-inlaid floors,
side galleries with books of law,
theology and the humanities...
a statue in the square of João III,
famous curfew-signalling
clock of Coimbra.

Black-caped students,
colored ribbons flying in the breeze,

identify their chosen professions...
walk by a stream that once flowed red
with the blood of Ines de Castro,
crowned queen of Portugal,
after her death,
by King Pedro I.

In a drenching downpour
we first view Fatima...
a huge stadium-size square
of wet concrete,
site of world-famous pilgrimages.
The Chapel of the Apparitions
to the left,
halfway on the square,
overflows
every May 13 and October 13
as pilgrims choke the road with traffic.

The square is almost empty
this afternoon in late April.
Stairs lead up the hill
to a cold white basilica.
At the center of the square
the tree stands preserved,
where the Virgin Mary
appeared to Lucia and her cousins,
Jacinto and Francisco.
A fountain flows at the spot
Lucia was asked to dig for water,
water that gushed into a stream.
The Lady made six appearances in 1917,
the first one May 13
and the last one October 13.
The three children,
joined by seventy thousand persons,
all witnessed

The Miracle of the Sun.
In the accelerating crowds,
only the three children saw The Lady.

Here and there we see
men and women doing penance,
walking on their knees
up the stairs to the sacred statue
of Our Lady of Fatima.

Under umbrellas
we walk to the basilica,
attend afternoon mass at three,
emerge to a world washed clean,
welcome shimmering sunshine,
stop to buy a book,
*The Story of Fatima.*

We are on our way
to the Province of Ribatejo
in the heartland of Portugal.
The River Tagus,
originating in Spain,
overflows its banks in winter…
bluegrass, Arabian horses
and black bulls,
Campinos in stocking caps,
sturdy horsemen of the region
as brave as their bulls.
Sounds of horses' hooves
and rumbling bulls
reverberate in the village streets
at *festa* time,
says a handout leaflet.

Our next dwelling
is the Pousada de São Pedro,

near Portugal's largest reservoir lake
and power-generating plant
in the forest by the City of Tomar.

We walk down the hill to the lake,
wander around its perimeter
cool and green in the waning light,
walk back to the *pousada*
and linger in the garden until dark.
Large windows overlook the lake
clustered with sailboats
and fishing boats.

Clarinda, suffering from a cold,
sips a bourbon-on-the-rocks,
goes to bed without dinner.
The remaining four of us
enjoy a leisurely meal,
partake of sweets of Abrantes
mentioned in the brochures,
conclude they mean the desserts
displayed in a glass-enclosed
cart that greets diners as
they enter the dining room,
tempting them beyond endurance.

I retire to read *The Fatima Story*,
mindful of shopping in Tomar
the next morning.

The City of Tomar
was bound to the Knights Templar,
militant monks
of wealth and power,
who began constructing in 1160
the Convent of Christ
on a tree-covered hill,

Nana's
Kiss-Me Cake

*Bolo de Beijar-Me*

*page 170*

surrounded by a walled castle.
The Knights fought the Arabs
at Santarem.
The pope suppressed
their misused power in 1314.
The Knights had made many enemies
of those who coveted their riches.
King Dinis ordered their regrouping
into a new Order of Christ.
Henrique the Navigator,
their famous Grand Master,
subsidized his explorations
with Templar money.

We find the stores in Tomar closed.
I ask a woman strolling by
if it is a holiday.
"This is Portugal's Independence Day,
proclaimed April 25, 1974,"
she answers.

Later I read that they overthrew
Dictator Caetano that day,
the successor to Dictator Salazar.
Much like our own 4th of July,
people gather in every village
to celebrate in public places,
return to their private homes
to continue the celebration.

In the village square,
we visit St. John the Baptist Church
of black-and-white diamond mosaics,
built by King Manuel I
in the 15th Century...
a white-and-gold baroque altar,
a chapel of aquamarine tiles.

The back of the church opens to
narrow cobbled streets and shops.
Above Tomar streets,
flowers in flowerpots hang
from wrought-iron-enclosed balconies.

The map indicates we enter
the Province of Alentejo,
plain of fire and ice,
also in the heartland of Portugal.
Whitewashed houses with tiny windows
keep out the freezing winter
and the scorching summers.

Often as we ride along
we talk of our homes,
my daughter Julie in San Francisco,
my son Edward
and our Aunt Amelia
both in Sacramento,
Mary's family in the Delta,
and Clarinda's family in Idaho.

"I especially like what Frank said,"
Clarinda remembers...
"I won't miss what Diane does for us,
we can do those things ourselves.
I will just miss Diane very much."

Evora, Beja, Vila Vicosa,
Castelo de Vide,
we drive not always
the most direct route...
more interesting this way.

The springtime countryside
keeps changing

up and down over spreading hills,
outcroppings of rocks,
yellow forsythia,
some yellow bell flowers
shaped much like lupine,
olive orchards and budding grapes,
star-shaped white flowers,
fruit trees in bloom,
huge vivid pink fernlike trees
suspended between grass and sky,
our car the only vehicle on the road.

I savor the quiet,
relax in the warm sunshine,
utterly at peace with myself
and the world around us.

All at once I feel breathless,
an almost overpowering
sense of glee…
waves of excitement
rush up my spine,
a feeling as if I am coming home.
Something is happening to me,
something I don't understand.
I say nothing, wondering,
trying to sort it out.
It is as if I have been here before.
Unable to no longer contain myself,
I gush on and on
about the wonders
of our surroundings.
So enthralled are we
that Maria forgets her camera.
Oh well, she never could have gotten
my feeling on film.

High ahead of us
on a distant mountaintop
appears a gleaming white castle.
"Ooh, let's be sure to explore
that tomorrow," I say,
"whatever it is."

We follow a POUSADA sign
with arrows pointing up a mountain.
"Looks awfully steep to me,"
says Maria.
Assuring her that we can make it,
we become aware
that the white castle
still far above us
is our *pousada* destination.
This is beyond my wildest imagination,
I keep thinking,
charged like a volt of magic.

We start the winding climb
to the 13th-Century
Castelo de Santa Maria
within the walled town
of Marvão.

Leaving the car at the entrance,
we take the narrow cobblestone
streets to the office
climbing, walking, climbing,
notice parked cars on a side lot.
Now we know it can be driven.
Diane and Maria walk back
and bring the car to us.
We drive up, up, and up
to the office at the top
peak of the Serra de São Mamede.

"Mom, since you love this place,
you three take the higher room,"
says Diane.
Standing on the balcony
I can see forever.
Making the sign of the cross
north, south, east and west,
I ask a blessing on Planet Earth
and on all of us on it.

Sipping cool spring water
from pottery mugs
poured from a pottery pitcher,
we rest, contemplating
the panorama before our eyes.

Revived, we stroll the castle ruins,
watch the sun go down.
Extreme cold drives us indoors
to warm up with before-dinner drinks
in the afterglow.
We dine by a blazing fire.

Tired, but too elated to sleep,
I indulge in my favorite pastime,
thinking and reminiscing.
Slowly, things seem
to start making sense
this night in Marvão
in the white castle
Pousada of Santa Maria.

I remember a strange dream
I dreamed last year
after a good tiring day
raking piles and piles
of autumn leaves,

absorbing the shades of color
from green to yellow to red
as I sloshed in them
to my heart's content.
The dream came with an urgent
message…"Time to go…
time to go…time to go…"
it repeated much like
an old record with its needle
stuck in a groove.
I could not decipher
my haunting dream,
decided clarity would come later…
it always does.

Now I realize
it was soon after
that I had decided
the coming new year
would be the right time
to visit the Azores Island
and even went so far
as to phone the travel agency.

Now I know it was Ed,
my husband,
nudging me from eternity
with the time-to-go message.
And it was his voice,
a sort of baritone quality
that I could never forget…
nothing new…
in these twenty-five years
I have received
many mental messages
but never see them as such
until long after I act upon them.

Usually, they come wrapped in
a *saudades* sort of longing.
Yet, I have been dismissing them
as ideas that pop into my mind.

It was he who nudged
our daughters and maybe even
my sister and my cousin
just so I would not travel alone.
He knows
sentimental journeys
must be shared
with special someones
or other loved ones.

Finally, tired after a busy day,
a day of adventure,
a night of putting things together,
I fall into a very deep sleep.

Dressed in a gossamer gown
of flowing rainbow colors
with ribbons tying
the dark curly hair
of my youth,
I walk up a rugged hill
in dainty slippers,
darting from rock to rock,
to a white castle at the top.

A young man, wearing leather
breeches and boots,
a white shirt with ruffled cuffs,
a falcon on his arm,
walks out the castle door.
He studies the sky
as he releases the bird.

The falcon flies to freedom
as the man gazes longingly after it.

Then he sees me,
pauses, smiles, and waits.
I rush to him.
He gathers me in his arms.
We dance as in a ballet.
Over the grass he pursues me.
In a whirlwind of urgency
we dance into the mist
spreading over the mountain…
spin away from each other
and back together again,
swirl and twirl
completely in rhythm,
a rhythm that hints
of ultimate perfection.

The mist thickens
creating chaos
disturbing our togetherness.
My man disappears.
I call and call
but cannot find him anywhere.
Enveloped in the mist,
I weep.
My dress feels damp
as I search in an urgency
of *saudades*.

Suddenly, I feel his arms
around me again.
Back in the mist we frolic.
I dance away…
but not too far.
He pursues me.

I, the pursued,
swerve, and pursue him.

We spin around the castle
into the emerging sunshine,
into a meadow
strewn with flowers
and nectar-sipping butterflies.
He whirls me
and the rainbow colors
of my flowing dress
high above his head.

Back into the shelter of his arms,
I hear him whisper in my ear,
"You know I could never
ever leave you."

Savoring the bliss
of the sacred moment,
gradually I float far away
back to reality
and awaken alone.

The sun on the balcony
bids me welcome.
I lie in a daze
contemplating my dream.
I say nothing about it
to Clarinda or Mary.
It is a treasure
to keep locked in my heart,
a source of joy
in my return to reality.

Later I will deal
with the enticing prospects

of future jaunts
back into eternity.

We breakfast,
cash traveler's checks at the *banco*,
purchase stamps at the *correio*,
and say farewell
to my *pousada* of happiness.

Past Portalegre
the road becomes more crowded.
Road work in progress
reroutes us elsewhere.
Clarinda warns Maria
of the danger of driving
between two tank trucks ahead,
most likely carrying gasoline.
At the first chance,
Maria passes both vehicles.
We notice the word VINHO
on the sides of both trucks.
"Oh well," quips Diane,
"if an accident happened,
the wine fumes would surely get us."

We miss a turn,
end up on a rugged country road,
see a few women in the fields,
kerchiefs covering their hair,
working alongside the men.
Since this is April,
we see no harvest of crops,
only some spring cultivation
and planting.

We stop to ask a farmer
the way to the main road.

Unconsciously, the three of us
ask at the same time.
He gestures for silence,
asks that we talk one at a time.
We abandon the contest to Mary.
I start giving Diane instructions.
"Mom, you're talking to me
in Portuguese," she protests.
Clarinda explains the way
in a calm tone in English.
We finally find the main highway.

As mentioned in the brochure,
we spot some cork trees.
"Remember," I say,
"In Sunny Slope School, we learned
that Portugal's main exports
are wine and cork."
Clarinda remembers.
We stop to examine a lone tree
growing by the roadside,
peel off some cork bark
as souvenirs.

Past Aviz and Monteforte,
we head for Estremoz,
a white pyramid in the center
of a marble quarry region,
rising out of the plains of Alentejo
to the Pousada de Rainha Isabel,
named for the wife of King Dinis...
a palace of spacious rooms,
red-jeweled-print canopies
over our beds
with drapes to match,
antique furniture, tapestries,
medieval red velvet and damask,

crystal, silver, and gold...
I get the feeling that every room,
every wall, every object,
every jardiniere in every courtyard
is steeped in history.

We dine on fettucini Alfredo
cooked with an elegant flourish
at our table
in the formal dining room.

Estremoz is the only town in our tour
beset by begging youths.
A band of boys and a pretty girl,
all about twelve years old,
surround our car,
guide us to a parking place,
and ask for escudos and dollars.

Diane and Maria honor their appeals
and other beggars gather around.
Dressed in clean denims
and tee shirts,
they know exactly when to smile,
how to turn on the tears,
how to disappear
when hotel personnel come
to get the bags of guests.

An older man and woman watching
with disapproval on their faces
assure us the beggars are not Portuguese
because Portuguese children
are always well behaved, they say.
The beggars are Gypsies,
able to speak whatever language
their hoped-for beneficiaries speak.

Two older women guests about to leave
are surrounded by the beggars
asking for escudos and dollars.
"Why aren't you in school?"
asks one.
"Because, Madam,"
replies one of the boys,
"today is Saturday."

We leave Estremoz early
for the long run south
to the Algarve,
stop at the Village of Arraiolos,
famous since the 13th Cenutry
for Persian-like rugs
handmade of heavy wool
tinted with natural dyes
and elaborate intricate designs
of every imaginable color.
I purchase several chairmats.
Maria and Mary buy rugs.
At a nearby shop, we get two sets
of Monopoly in Portuguese
for the little Azorean cousins.
We buy chicken pies
in the village cafeteria,
eat them in the grassy square
sitting under budding trees.

Driving over the mountains
past valleys full of wild flowers,
acres of yellow forsythia,
we arrive in Alportel
and the Pousada de São Bras.

São Bras,
an isolated hilltop villa

in the surrounding *serras*
by a fig orchard with painted stones,
bids us welcome in many languages.

Breathing air
that is a treat to breath,
we find complete tranquility,
as promised in the brochures...
another forever view
from the balcony
of our second-floor rooms,
time to relax for two days,
time to have our laundry done,
time to send cards
to my sisters in Idaho...
Marie, Dorothy, Patty, Ellen,
and to Naomi in Sacramento...
a full day to visit the Algarve.

On a table in the lounge
among the usual Portuguese newspapers,
wonder of wonders,
a paper and a magazine in English...
Maria grabs *USA Today*.
I am the first to reach *Newsweek*,
sit and read by the fire
as we drink hot coffee.
"Mom, you don't have to read
every word," says Diane,
awaiting her turn.

Clarinda orders only soup for dinner,
sharing my entree of liver and onions,
a much-too-generous serving.

"I certainly miss ice,"
says Maria. "What they call

chilled is only cold."
I remind her that ice
no longer exists after one leaves
the U.S.A. It is an American luxury.

"A good cup of coffee
is what I would like to find,"
says Clarinda.
"The coffee is too strong
and it's served in tiny cups.
I keep asking for a larger cup
and a pot of hot water.
Even when I dilute it,
it is still too strong."

"I wish someone knew
what cooked cereal is," says Mary.
"I have to explain at every
breakfast. Some call it porridge
and the next place doesn't
know what porridge is."

As for me, I tell them,
"I miss a lunch, or a dinner place
for that matter, where I can
order just a snack.
I am tired of ordering meals
with more food than I want.
In fact, I'm determined
to eat about the same amounts
I eat at home."

"Speak for yourself, Mother,"
says Maria, adding,
"Diane, you're the only one
not complaining about the food."

"I haven't thought about it.
Give me time to think,"
laughs Diane.

"You haven't changed,"
remembers Maria.
"You never used to ask for treats
like candy or ice cream
like the rest of us...guess
that's why you never gain a pound."

Three young men
speaking a little English
approach Diane and Maria.
"Mom," calls Diane
from across the dining room.
I interpret for them.
Representatives of a firm in Lisbon,
they work in various villages.
Maria tells them of her work
in a television studio.
Diane tells of hospital work.
The State of California
they know very well.
They are interested in America.

I wonder what there is about us
that no matter where we go,
everyone recognizes
that we are American.

We return to the lounge
to sit in front of the fire.
"Let me read you my notes
on where we'll be tomorrow,"
I say.

Everyone gets comfortable,
ready to listen.

The Algarve
the Garden of Portugal
southwesternmost part of Europe,
one hundred miles
of Atlantic coastline,
starts at Cape Santo Vincente
of Henrique the Navigator,
north to Vila Real de Santo Antonio
at the Spanish border.

Legend has it that a handsome
and sensitive Arab vizier
in the Moorish town of Xelb,
a city now called Silves,
wed a Nordic young princess.

Living in the rose castle,
she longed for snow-covered hills
and the valleys of her native land.
The vizier had thousands of almond
trees planted in his kingdom.
The princess rejoiced every winter
at the white blossoms and fragrance,
and they lived happily ever after.

Summer reigns all year
in the valleys south of the hills.
Pale blue sky
deepens to a vivid blue by evening.
In the countryside grow lemons,
pomegranates, oranges and carob,
and the ten thousand almond trees
of the legend.
Octopus-like tentacled branches

of fig trees
crawl across the orchards.
Geraniums of every color adorn
the roadsides
from Sagres to Lagos.

Golden sands,
sun-drenched beaches,
sky-etched black boulders,
in-rushing ocean waters
carving caves and grottos,
sheltered lagoons
and evergreen woods
invade foam-capped waves
pounding the Atlantic turf.

The earthquake of 1755
left Roman and Moorish ruins.

In coastal fishing villages,
a leaflet mentions
bullfighters of the Atlantic,
in black embroidered apparel
with flowers in their hats,
as the living tradition
in a land well known
to seafaring Romans,
Visigoths, Greeks, Phoenicians,
Moors and Christians,
today also well known to the many
flying foreign visitors.

Before the fire burns itself out,
we retire to our rooms
to dream of the Algarve.

Sagres, Lagos, Portimão,
Praia da Rocha, Silves,
Armacão de Pera, Faro,
Albufeira, Vilamoura...
we drive into and through towns
more or less as the birds fly,
often retracing our routes,
not always following the map,
stopping haphazardly
where imagination leads.

We become aware
of Mary's extensive travels
as throughout our tour
she utters as we pass
certain castles and villages,
"I was here once."

Steep cliffs jut out
into the Atlantic
at the extreme southwesterly
corner of Portugal
at Sagres.
Here Henrique the Navigator,
of the creative, exploring mind,
established his
School of Navigation...
now a youth hostel...
launched his dreams
for his country and the world
upon the seas of exploration.

Three miles into the sunset
over the edge of the world
a lighthouse sits
at Cape Santo Vincente...
trees bent from gusty winds,

seagulls glide on currents…
the last explored point known
to the ancient world.

Lagos
an ancient seaport
traced back to the Carthaginians,
back to 300 B.C.
Sailors of Nelson's English fleet
told of lovely olive-skinned
green-eyed women
of the Algarve…
called Zawaia by the Moors,
Locobriga by the Lusitanians…
the Bay of Sagres
on the Costa de Ouro,
the Coast of Gold,
once was filled with warships.

We stroll on a mountain walkway
high above the sunny beach.
I buy a white woolen sweater
edged in turquoise and rose,
cap and scarf to match.
We find a hole-in-the-wall eatery
for a mid afternoon meal,
prawns for Mary and Maria,
grilled sole for Clarinda,
Diane and me,
the best we have yet tasted.

In the evening we return
to the Pousada de São Bras
to a quiet supper,
to dream by the fire,
to sleep off our weariness
from a day that sped by

filled with interesting
unusual places and things.
There is a lot to sort out.

Diane, Mary, and I attend mass early
while the others sleep.
We cannot find our way back
even though we see the *pousada*
on a hill. We cannot find
the street leading to it. In every
street, we encounter some obstacle.
A man on a motorcycle
with a little boy behind him
approaches us.
I roll down the window,
ask him the way to São Bras.
"Follow me," he says,
leading us right to it.
I offer the child
an American dollar.
The man declines it,
explains the *tourisimo* agency
hires him to look out
for stranded tourists.
"I guess they really mean it
when they advertise *tourisimo*,"
says Diane.

We do many personal tasks,
write cards to friends,
walk in the forest,
drive the countryside to Faro
nestled at the foot
of the Serra de Caldeirão,
a garden of flowers.

From a ceramics factory
we find in the country,
we purchase platters and plates
designed in shades of blue,
flat pieces that we can easily
pack among our clothes.

Almost every other night
Diane phones home, talks
to Frank and Jim and Angel.
One call costs eighty dollars.
She says it is worth it.
Maria phones Tom,
gives him the telephone number
and he phones back at once.
They save money that way.
Diane and Maria check
international time schedules,
calculate when to phone.
Portugal is eight hours ahead
of California time.

I find in the *pousada* library
a novel printed in English…
*Humboldt's Gift* by Bellow…
become engrossed in it,
read in front of the fire
after dinner, and again in bed,
propped up on pillows,
until my eyes almost give out,
around past three in the morning.

We drive from São Bras
in Southeastern Portugal
across the Arrabida Mountains
through pine groves
to the Land of the Three Castles

Sesimbra, Setubal, and Palmela,
through the Tagus and Sado Valleys
to the sea.
Orchards of ripening oranges
and muscatel vineyards
make me wish it were September
as I remember the taste
of the muscatel grapes
growing on my hilltop acre
in California.

My remembering
triggers thoughts of home.
Clarinda wonders
if her sons properly pet the calves,
talk to them in loving words
as they feed them milk.
"Statistics compiled
by the dairy association,"
she informs us,
"prove that calves raised by women
thrive far better."

We pass architectural remnants
of the Moors, the Phoenicians,
and the Romans, plus the Spanish
reminders of the earthquake.

We reach the last *pousada*
on our tour, at the foot
of the Arrabida Mountains,
Palmela...
site of a Celt Castle in 300 B.C.
and the Palmela Castle
of the 12th Century
from where Alfonso I,

the first king of Portugal,
drove out the invading Moors.

*Pousada* signs lead to our destination,
the Pousada do Castelo de Palmela,
a converted nunnery
overlooking the valleys and the sea.
Cells with hand-carved furniture,
blue tile baths,
and velvet, satin, brocade fabrics
have become our bedrooms.
We dine in the elegant dining room
where once nuns sang soft chants.

"Since we go to Lisbon tomorrow,
let me read to you all about it,"
I say, unfolding pages
retrieved from my luggage,
also gleaned from my
extensive research.

Lisbon
was known as
the eighth wonder of the world
in its golden age…
the hub of trade
between Europe and Africa and Asia
in the 1500s…
a bazaar displaying
treasures from the Orient…
porcelains, silks, rubies, pearls,
diamonds and other gemstones,
indigo and spices…
and from the Americas
Brazilwood, coffee and gold.

Lisboa…Lisbon
destroyed in the Great Earthquake
at mass time in the morning
of All Saints Day, 1755…
trapped worshipers tried to flee
as violence of the sea smashed
anchored vessels in the harbor.
Thousands of people drowned.

Ignited by fallen candles
in homes and churches,
fierce winds of flames and ashes
covered streets, parks, and squares.
Houses tangled with fallen roofs
and separated foundations
all crumbled in heaps of rubble.

Thousands of people perished,
crushed under scattered debris
of public buildings,
royal palaces and town houses,
fisherman cottages and cathedrals.
Few structures remained standing.
Fire consumed the City in six days.

Walls of water
over forty feet high
from the Tagus and the sea
washed the ravaged, burned remains.

The new Lisboa,
almost like an unplanted tree,
grew from the ashes
on the right bank
of the River Tagus…
a monument on the left bank
of Christ with arms outstretched…

the westernmost capital
of Continental Europe.

Pastel-washed houses
and red tile roofs
capture the sun's warmth
and dazzle the eyes.
Black-and-white mosaics
form arabesques on sidewalks
and on paved area
approaches of buildings.
Ponte 25 de Abril,
largest suspension bridge in Europe,
spans the Tagus River,
a replica of Golden Gate Bridge
in San Francisco Bay, U.S.A.

Lisbon is the birthplace
of Portugal's favorite saint,
Santo Antonio de Padua,
patron of the poor,
theologian,
defender of human rights.

Entering the New Lisbon
we find our lodging,
the Palace Avenida Hotel
on the Rua de Dezembro.
We wait at a busy intersection
across the street,
knowing we must turn left
against oncoming cars.

A woman approaches,
carrying a shopping bag,
a loaf of crusty bread protruding.
She sees our car

filled with five women
waiting in the wild traffic.
She stops, hesitates,
and blesses herself.

Miraculously,
we make it to the hotel,
park and settle in
for a two-day stay.
We shop on the Rua de Ouro
for gold chains
to adorn our necks,
buy strawberries from a cart
on a busy street corner.

From the Castle of St. George,
Castelo de São Jorge,
we see the City spread out
to the river and hills beyond
as we stand beside a statue
of King John I in armor
riding his horse.

Fish in Tomato
Sauce

*Piexe em Molho
de Tomate*

*page 157*

We enjoy lunch
in the kind of restaurant we seek,
a hole-in-the-wall one.
Mary and I order dry codfish
in a tomato sauce,
reminiscent of our mothers'
Friday night suppers.
I don't like it any better.
It still tastes like straw.
But the tasty sauce suffices
served on bits of crusty bread.

We buy ornamental tiles,
embroidered blouses and dirndls.

Maria and Diane get
an entry-hall rug of many colors
for their sister Julie.
In a narrow back street,
we watch two buses approach
each other, no room to pass.
Each stops to weigh the situation.
Slowly they pass each other
with hardly an inch to spare.
As wild as driving appears…
eyes searching for street names
printed on sides of buildings,
cars parked on sidewalks,
cars passing each other
completely at random,
we witness no accidents.
Guardian Angels
must surely be in charge.

We stroll in the park
dominated by a monument
of famous Portuguese explorers,
the Memorial of the Discoveries.
Henrique and De Gama,
a man holds a cross,
navigators, monks,
cartographers, cosmographers
stand at the top of the prow
of a ship tipped with their weight,
bearing the coat of arms
of Manuel I…
all immortalized in stone
where the Tagus River
flows to the sea.

We set out to tour
the Museum of Archeology,

its ancient jewelry
and sculptures of 2000 B.C.
days of the Visigoths...
the Coach Museum
displaying fairy-tale coaches
of the 17th, 18th, and 19th Centuries,
founded by Queen Amelia...
the Museum of Popular Art,
the National Art Gallery,
the private art collection
of Calouste Gulbenkian Museum...
all enticingly described
in the brochures.
To our dismay,
they are closed, every one.
It is May Day,
the Portuguese Labor Day.
Oh well, maybe next time...

At sunset and twilight,
we tour Lisbon by bus,
ending in the oldest section,
the Alfama...
pass crooked cobbled streets,
tilting houses
almost touching each other,
mingle with the confusion
of bars and shops
within old Visigoth walls,
enter a Fado Club.

*Fados*
folk songs of sorrow
of nostalgia
of love and longing
of life and fate...
the perfect songs of *saudades*.

What has been ordained is,
and nothing can be done.
The *Rubáiyát* comes to mind...
"The moving finger writes
and having writ
moves on—
nor all thy piety nor wit
shall lure it back to cancel half a line
nor all your tears
wash out a word of it."

Singers clutch black shawls
as they pour out in song,
in tender whispers
and wailing laments,
songs of past loves,
sing of past glories
of the empire gone forever...
accompanied by a guitar
and a viola.

The poignancy of "Lisboa"
rivals the words we know,
"I left my heart
in San Francisco."
I am also reminded
of the World War II song,
"The Last Time I Saw Paris."

We and the singer
become as one,
develop a sort of kinship
to be remembered forever
with *saudades*...
songs of *saudades*.

Ed would have loved them,
would have been tempted
to return another day
to blend their haunting songs
with the plaintive tones
of his clarinet
or even his saxophone.

Our hotel room absorbs
street noises day and night.
Longing for the *pousadas*
on quiet mountaintops,
I drift off to sleep,
thinking of many things…
dream we are in a church
filled with mostly women,
many of them wearing black,
widows in mourning
for the rest of their lives.

Back to reality at morning mass
the congregation seems restless.
I have difficulty understanding
the Gospel and the sermon.
The words move too fast.
Maria and Clarinda leave at once.

A herd of cattle
won't let our car pass.
Driving in the mountains
in a cloudburst
our dusty car gets washed.
We pass an oxen-pulled cart
with a man and a woman in it
bringing home a load of firewood.
Maria keeps filming our journey
everywhere we go…

We attempt to pronounce
the names of the villages.
<u>A</u> sounds like <u>ah</u>.
<u>E</u> sounds like <u>ay</u>.
<u>I</u> sounds like <u>ee</u>.
<u>O</u> in the body of a word
sounds like the word <u>awe</u>.
<u>O</u> at the end of a word
sounds like <u>ooh</u>,
<u>ão</u> sounds like <u>oan</u> with little <u>n</u> sound.
<u>U</u> sounds like <u>oo</u> in <u>book</u>,
and there is no <u>W</u> and no <u>Y</u>.

Half-awake, I wonder
was it in Alcaçar, Gavião,
Estoril or Portalegre
a sunny day in April
as we motored on a narrow
winding cobblestone estrada
that I saw in a tiny window
of a scarred ancient wall
the face of a young woman?

Her wistfulness reminded me
of Sundays on the ranch,
my child face in the window,
longing for each passing car
to turn into our lane.

I caught her eye, hesitated,
then smiled and waved.
All at once, she glowed.
A warmth flowed through me.
I, the foreigner,
felt kin to her that instant
and to every passerby.

Looking back, I wonder if she
felt the same kinship as I.

On the plane the next day,
we watch Portugal fade from sight,
swallowed by the Atlantic…
mentally waft *amor e adeus,*
love and goodbye,
hoping we return someday.

*Saudades…Saudades…*

*Return to
Azorean Adventure*

On TAP Flight 197Y
to Ponta Delgada,
we approach
the Island of São Miguel,
fly over an unapproachable-
looking coastline of black boulders.

From the Hotel Canadian,
in a minibus
with an English-speaking guide
who has shortened his name
of Antonio to Tony, we tour first
the Pinhal de Paz Park.

Pink azalea trees bloom
in fresh green leaves
etched against azure skies.
Natives of South America,
solar hot-house pineapples grow
in peat moss hauled from the mountains.
Signs point out Isabella grapevines
from North America,
cactus yellow flowers of Indian figs
from Mexico,
tea plants, cha, from the Orient.

Wild calla lilies and daisies
in woodland meadows and hillside fields
charm the eye.
Elephant Ears of taro roots
grow in marshy areas.

Subtropical vegetation forms a jungle
in nearby Terra Nostra Park.

Maria films a procession.
Over azalea-strewn streets,
a priest carries
a cross covered with blooms,
followed by little boys in white suits,
little girls in pastel dresses,
into the ornate Church of São Bras,
baroque with Azorean imprint,
successor to the early settler
Church of Nosa Senhora de Rosario.

Tony, our guide, turns out to be
a marvelous source of information
about the Islands
and their relationship
with Portugal.
We ask many questions.
He tells us he feels
the Continentals don't realize
that democracy and freedom
entail responsibility, adding,
"They think democracy means
they can do anything they wish
even if it hurts someone else."

In all fairness,
I must add
the Continentals wonder
why we would want to visit
the Azores Islands.
They intimate and assume
all foreign tourists
seek jet-set entertainment,
not realizing that for us

it is a plus to see
the beauty of the islands
unspoiled by commercialism.

We drive into the mountains
to see Sete Citades,
Seven Cities,
legendary center of a mighty empire
in Atlantis.
We stop at a vista point to see
Lago Verde e Azul,
Lake Green-Blue,
formed by the teardrops
shed over a broken love affair
between a blue-eyed princess
and a green-eyed shepherd boy.

Gardens surround white stucco houses
with red tile roofs,
terraced with stones and walls
as protection against erosion.
Oxen-pulled plows cultivate
steep mountainsides,
and tractors cultivate lowland plots.
On roadways, oxen-pulled carts
mingle with automobiles.

In another part of the Island,
hot, sulfurous geysers cloud
rocks covered with yellow deposits.
Poor villagers save on energy
by cooking in cloth bags
fish and potatoes
in the boiling turbulent waters.

Tony arranges for Maria
to visit the local TV station

in the evening.
She and Diane talk with the crew,
Tony interpreting.
"They have the same spirit
of friendship and rivalry
as we have at our TV studio,"
says Maria, "but their equipment
and facilities are many years
behind ours. It was interesting
to see how we must have done it
before my time."

We return the next morning
to Ponta Delgada Aeroporto,
are joyfully reunited
with my sister Marie
and brother-in-law Cam,
who interrupted their tour of Spain
to join us for a few days.
We seven board the inter-island
plane with the Rolls-Royce symbol,
and we are on our way
to the Island of Pico.

We glimpse the volcano,
Pico's cone in brilliant sunlight
suspended in the sky,
the rest hidden in the mist.

Gloria and her family
and an assortment of cousins
welcome us at the *aeroporto.*
I assume the role
of chief interpreter,
introducing our four new members...
same smiles and same misty eyes,
European kiss on each cheek...

searches for luggage,
hauling bags into metal carts,
pushing carts to waiting
cars and Amaro's truck.
"Don't forget the box of pineapples,
special ones from São Miguel."

Fortunately for Diane and Maria,
they are assigned to the car
of English-speaking Fernando,
a friend of Gloria's family.

Clarinda and I marvel
at the springtime growth
that has transpired
in the two weeks we were gone.
The volcanic rock fences
around the plots
are no longer visible,
covered with grapevines,
blooming fruit trees,
and greening shrubs in bloom.
Everywhere we look
we see riots of color.
Our mother did not exaggerate
when she told us about
her flower-strewn island.

In Gloria's house and courtyard,
lively conversation
keeps Clarinda and Mary and me
busily interpreting,
in spite of fatigue, mixing
words of Portuguese and English.

I realize someone is missing.
"I haven't seen Mara.

Where is she?" I ask.
Fatima tells us
Mara has the measles.
"It is a blow to her
that she cannot join us."

We visit Mara
in the basement sewing room,
lying on a bed,
her face blotchy and reddened.
"We decided it is best for her
to be away from everyone, and
I sleep on the other bed,"
says Gloria, fluffing the pillow.

We greet a subdued Mara,
give her a trinket
we purchased in Portugal,
tell her about the Monopoly game
we brought for her and Marilia.

"Is it all right if we visit her?"
asks Clarinda.
"Yes, anytime," says Fatima.
"We'll just pop in anytime,"
I say.  Mara manages a smile.

Marilia tells us that a cousin
will stay with Mara
while we are gone the remainder
of the day.

After a refreshing lunch,
brief rests in our rooms,
we explore the outdoors,
sit on the balcony
and gaze at the Atlantic

stretching to the northern horizon,
at one with the sounds of the sea,
waves splashing the rocky shore…
for Clarinda and Mary and me
a welcome repetition,
for the others
the charm of a new experience.

Gloria announces,
"We are spending the rest of the day
at Terra Alta."
We scatter for wraps
needed for the cold of the evening,
set forth for an hour's uphill walk.

Jose Lourenco and Aurea
and their three children…
Maria Luis, Lourenco, Rubene…
join us for the festivities and walk.
Silverio and Maria,
Arminda and Helio
will join us later for dinner.

Green grapevines climb over
black volcanic rock fences.
Relentless rhythmic waves creep up
smooth shoreline ebony boulders,
retreating to the sea on our left.
We hike the hills this day in May
to the *adega* in late afternoon…
azalea-bordered stony roadway
invaded with calla lilies,
pink moss flowers, clumps of daisies.
Children pluck and toss petals.
"He loves me.  He loves me not.
He remains indifferent."

We enter the *adega* we remember.
Amaro leads us
to the basement wine room,
pours Angelica from a barrel on its side
into pottery cups for a toast to us.
"*A Saude*,"
"Our Good Health."
Heady sips of fragrant wine blend
with the get-acquainted words
of the new American cousins.

At the seashore just before sunset,
we remove our shoes, take knives
and wade in to pry tiny lapis
clinging to the ancient rocks.
We toss them into wicker baskets.
Some islanders remove one shell
and scoop the morsel from the other,
consuming them on the spot.
I opt to wait for cooked ones later.

We trudge uphill at twilight
to the *adega*, our gathering done,
assemble for a candlelight *festa*…
aromas of fish and oysters
swimming in delicate sauces
vie with linguiça, inhames, torresmos,
cooked greens, red Pico wine,
and fruit cup floating in Angelica.

We Pacific-oriented Americans
walk back late that night
hand-in-hand in the dark
with our Atlantic relatives
to the Village of Santo Amaro.

Pork in Wine &
Garlic

*Torresmos*

*page 162*

The full moon lights the roadway,
caresses the waves now on our right,
lapping the rock-silhouetted shoreline.
I sense our departed parents smiling
that a generation later we return
to fortify the centuries-old family
ties to our Portuguese cousins.

"Today we go on a *piquenique*,"
says Fatima, assembling utensils,
plates, forks, spoons,
into a large basket.
Playing Monopoly in Portuguese
around the table,
the children clap and cheer.
Competing with conversation,
I hear *avenidas* and *escudo*
transactions as I watch
Amaro pour wine into a jug.
Gloria and Fatima carefully
put into baskets various dishes
filled with picnic fare.
"I won't be able to go with you,"
says Gloria. "I'm staying with Mara."

We sit on a patchwork quilt
spread on a large mattress
on the bed of the truck
alongside baskets of food.
Silverio and Maria
and Arminda and Helio
follow us in their car.

Amaro drives to a mountainside park
on the other side of the Island,
removes piled-up stones that serve

as a gate at the entrance.
We troop into a green, grassy knoll.

On an embroidered white cloth
with a blanket underneath,
dishes of food are set...
hard rolls and cheese, sweet rolls,
codfish balls subtly seasoned
and still warm, sausages,
left-over oysters and sauce cooked
with rice, sliced pineapple, spice
sheetcake, fragile lacelike cookies
and the inevitable jug of red wine...
a layout to tempt our palates
as we sit and recline
on grassy inclines
and sun-warmed boulders.

"Since I'm the photographer,
I never get into the pictures.
So, how about taking over, Cam?"
asks Maria, handing him
the camera and equipment.
Cam obliges and records
for posterity Maria's interactions
with the others, capturing
her clowning and many moods.

All the families get together
for a day in the *serras*.
Again, Gloria stays with Mara.
Sea-level trees and shrubs
that grow at different elevations
gradually give way to each other
as the cars climb higher and higher
to treeless alpine mountains
covered with grasses,

jutting rocks covered with moss,
inactive, long-dead volcanos,
and underground networks of caves.
Mist plays hide-and-seek
with the sun.
"The mist changes so quickly,
I can hardly keep up
with the camera," says Maria.

We stop near a *lago*,
a lake reflecting the blue
of the sky,
to climb a mountain.
As we laboriously ascend,
Rubene and Lourenco,
with youthful exuberance,
climb up and back down
to stay even with us.
"I'd love to have them
on the farm," says Clarinda.

"It is too early for wildflowers.
They grow in every color,
with yellow predominating, all
over the *serra* valleys all summer
long," says Silverio.
"Next time, come in summer.
You just have to see them,"
says Fatima.

We make it to the top,
some needing assistance.
Maria films our trek all the way
and Cam photographs selectively.
I stumble over a large
protruding rock,

come down on its mossy cover
like landing on a feather pillow.

Goats on jutting rocks
on mountainsides
watch us without comment
as they chew their cuds.
Pico,
the volcano,
pays no attention,
haughtily and silently proclaims
that beauty itself justifies being.

I do not go with the others
the day they walk the village
to film our ancestral houses.
I am too exhausted from the tension
of interpreting,
sometimes in split-second precision.
This gives me time for quiet
conversation with Gloria.

"You mentioned having suffered
a bad back recently.
Tell me about it," I say.

"I kinked my back in some way
and suffered much pain.
The *medico* examined me
and prescribed painkillers.
They left me light-headed
and much confused.
Still the pain persisted
until I became bedridden."

She continues her story.
"I knew I needed a special

doctor or a special person,
one who could manipulate
the neck and spine.
The Island often has had people
with a gift for that."
I remember someone once saying
one of our grandmothers had it.

Gloria says she started praying
and meditating for the proper
person to come forth.
One day Amaro heard
that a new doctor had come
to the village.
He went to see him
and the doctor agreed to come.

"He examined my back, my neck,
arms, and leg muscles.
He placed a rolled-up cloth
between my teeth and said
I would feel pain
when he jerked my back.
After agonizing spasms,
I welcomed relief, not even
minding the resulting soreness."

"'I want you to sit up,' he said.
'I can't. Dear God, I can't.'
'Yes you can. I'll help you.'"

Gloria says that, with the *medico's* help,
she was able to slowly
lie on her back,
then sit up,
and finally stand on her feet.

He gave instruction for her
to alternate lying down
with sitting up,
standing up and walking.
She was to be careful
not to get her back out again,
but was to stay active.

The *medico* returned to give
her a treatment that sounds
to me like acupressure.
He pronounced her well
on the way to recovery.
"As for the painkillers,"
she says, "I walked to the ocean
and tossed them into the waves."

Gloria has no way of knowing
how long he will remain
on the Island.
She says she will always
be grateful
that he appeared
almost out of nowhere
to heal her.

Word passes around the next day
that a dance will be held
in the church square that evening
to honor the *Americanos*.
It has to be this evening
If Cam and Marie are to come.
Every evening is taken up
by our limited time.

First, the villagers show us
how to dance the Chamarita.

We practice the intricate steps.
A tall young dancer
calls in Portuguese
the folk-dance directions.

> Enter the Gentlemen
> Enter the Ladies
> Let's go to the center
> Gentlemen dance behind the Ladies
> Ladies out in front
> Gentlemen to the front
> Gentlemen revolve around the Ladies
> Push the chair
> Half-revolving
> Each Gentleman passes a Lady
> Back and Forth
> Gentlemen to the front
> Dance to the Center
> Ladies to the right
> Gentlemen to the left
> Close the circle
> Let go of hands
> Dance forward and leap
> Ladies pass the Gentlemen
>     to original positions
> Take arms and dance out

A young man and his wife
play music on violas.
An older man sets the rhythm
rubbing and hitting two seashells
one against the other.

We, the dancers, stop for a break,
sip Angelica from a good-luck cup
passed to each one in the circle.
The Chamarita ends
when we dance out into the night,
cheering and clapping.

We visit the whaling museum,
buy scrimshaw, the same ivory
whale tusk carvings that fascinated
President Kennedy, as mentioned
in a book at the display.
We touch the wood of a whaling boat
that appears much too small
to have sailed in so vast a sea,
where men of courage plied their trade.
A fisherman, poised with split-time
precision, hurled a harpoon
at a whale and went
for a Nantucket Sleighride...
a much-needed industry once
in the days of our grandfathers.

No longer does the cry
*BALEIA...BALEIA*
resound across the Island
when the blowing of a whale is sighted.
These mighty creatures of the deep
now our world rightfully protects.

We visit the old lighthouse
on a high promontory,
its base standing in an area
of small, sharp black rocks
carved into grotesque shapes
by the forces of the sea,
climb the spiral staircase
to the tower.
Intricate patterns
of geometric-shaped glass
give the illusion of revolving,
shooting beams of light
in daylight hours
that must be magnified

when electrically operated
on dark Atlantic nights
to warn ships
against submerged dangers
and protruding perils.

Resting on the balcony
after a hectic, busy morning,
we bask in the calmness of the sea
and easy rhythm of the waves.
Gloria says,
"I still think I'm dreaming.
For years and years
we had hoped that at least one
American cousin would visit us."

"And now," laughs Marie,
"you get seven of us at once."

"Yes, isn't it wonderful.
These are days I will never forget.
My only regret is that Mother
did not live to see the day."

"Our mother, too, spoke of coming,
that is, after the family had left
and she was alone. She couldn't
afford it before," says Clarinda.

"Yes," I remind her,
"but long before, when we were babies,
our father had passports ready
for the four of us to visit here,
but he died
and we never made the journey."

Reminiscing, I continue.
"Years later...I can still see
us at the kitchen table talking.
I promised Mama
that I would go with her
to visit her island.
But, before I could easily afford it,
she died."

"Mother and our grandmother
often spoke of it," says Gloria,
sighing, "but only the Lord
knew it was never to be."

"Cam and I had planned to stay
at the motel in Madalena,"
says Marie. "We thought seven
of us would be too many for you,
but it has worked out nicely."

"Never would I have allowed it,"
says Gloria. "At least once,
I wanted all my American family
under my roof, even though
Silverio has plenty of room
and wanted you to stay with them."

"We promised Silverio and Maria
that the next time we visit,
we will stay with them,"
says Marie.
She laughs as she tells us
what Silverio said at the picnic
when his wife protested
he was endangering his life
by eating too much
and drinking too much wine.

"So what? If I die,
I die delightfully satisfied."

"This is a dream come true,"
I say.
"I feel our parents and all
our ancestors are rejoicing with us…
a sort of meeting
in these moments
of the here and the hereafter."

Marie and Cam leave before us,
return to their tour of Spain,
tell us that in all their travels,
this is their first
emotional encounter. Says Cam,
"I wish I could converse leisurely
with each relative
in his or my language."

Weekday evenings after dinner,
the family watches on television
a story much like our soapees,
about wealthy Brazilians
in country estates,
much like our "Dynasty."
They watch American films
and other foreign films
with Portuguese captions.
I take too long at first
to read the captions, matching
the Portuguese words
with English conversation.
What really confuses us
is trying to read the captions
while listening to Italian,
French, or German films.

I have been waiting
for a chance to find
some of our ancestors
in the church records.
The person in charge works,
is available only evenings.
One late afternoon
we get word
the man will be in the church hall.
We hurry over.
Mary and I search with him
for familiar names
in records of baptisms,
marriage, and death.
The penmanship is superb.
I find my father and mother
and several grandparents.
Now I have dates to add
to names I already have.
Records reveal that ages of death
of most people are 80s and 90s.
I guess we come from hardy stock.

Unleavened
Cake-Bread

*Bolo do Forno*

*page 151*

Fascinated with Gloria's bread
and her kitchen and courtyard,
Maria arranges to film her
making the ancient *bolo*.

The next morning Gloria assembles
her large mixing pan,
corn flour and wheat flour.
"Shall I get it started now
ahead of time?" she asks.

"No, please don't.  Maria wants
to get it all," I urge,
leaving the room to awaken her.

"Maria, Gloria is ready
to start making the bread."

"I'll get right up," she says,
half-asleep.
Diane gets up, also.
Clarinda and Mary join us.

Gloria ties together four branches
about four feet long,
thick with green leaves,
she had gathered that morning
to make a broom.
She checks the fire
in the old wall oven.
The coals are hot enough.
She sweeps them
with the green broom
to a compartment below
the bottom of the oven
and closes the sliding doors.

She measures the corn flour,
pours boiling water over it
and stirs it vigorously,
talking all the while
as one of us interprets.
She measures and adds
the rest of the ingredients,
and kneads the mixture well.
Since this is unleavened bread,
she shapes it at once
into round loaves, flattens them
like one-inch-thick pancakes.

After flouring each bread
for ease of handling,

she scoops them, one at a time,
onto a spoon-shaped flat paddle,
slides the oven door open
and places them in the oven,
closes the sliding door
and checks the time.

While the *bolo* bakes,
Gloria uncovers a large bowl
she had kneaded earlier
of leavened bread.
She punches down the raised dough
and shapes it
into six round loaves
to raise while the *bolo* bakes.

Maria continues filming Gloria
cleaning the table,
washing utensils,
laying them in the gravel area
of the courtyard
to dry in the sun.

As soon as the *bolo* is baked,
Maria films its advent
from the oven,
one flat cake at a time,
loaded on the paddle,
and set on the table to cool.

The paddle's work continues
loading the leavened loaves
into the oven.

We break one *bolo* into pieces
to taste its bland nutrition.
Clarinda must have butter.

The rest of us like it as is.
There is something satisfying
about it that appeases hunger.

Gloria explains that *bolo*
has always been their quick bread,
much as our American pioneer
baking powder biscuits.

"It is only in the last few years
that bread has been for sale
in the village. Until then,
were it not for *bolo*," Gloria says,
"some people might have gone hungry
waiting for leavened bread to rise."

Maria also films Gloria taking
the wheat loaves from the oven.
"There is no satisfaction like
taking loaves of freshly baked
bread from the oven,"
Clarinda says.
"A work of art," I say.

What happens to the broom?"
asks Mary.
"It dries into firewood
for the next baking," answers Gloria,
"but whenever I use the old oven,
I get a certain satisfaction
baking in the same oven
our grandmothers baked in,
but then, the new oven
is so much more convenient."

"Gloria is the Julia Child
of Santo Amaro," says Diane.

Whole Wheat Bread

*Pão de Trigo*

*page 152*

*127*

Somewhere I have seen stone houses
like the ones on Pico Island,
but I cannot remember where.
One day it comes to me…
they are like the ones
in Cornwall,
the television setting
for the "Masterpiece Theater"
"Poldark" series.
Now I wonder if some
British Isles are volcanic
like some of the Azores Islands.


"I wish you could stay
for the *Festa do Espírito Santo*,"
we hear over and over again,
the festival in honor
of the Holy Spirit,
the Third Person
of the Blessed Trinity,
symbolized as a white dove.


Well we know the legend
handed down orally by our parents,
celebrated in our home.


In a famine centuries ago,
the people prayed and prayed
for deliverance from famine,
invoking the Holy Spirit.
One morning they sighted a ship
aground on the rocky shore,
a ship with no crew,
a ship full of all kinds of food,
food enough to tide them over
into the next harvest.

Since then in the Island of Pico
every year at Pentecost
fifty days after Easter
when the Holy Spirit
descended on the apostles,
the Holy Spirit is honored
in a Festa do Espírito Santo…
a special high mass
and a procession,
headed by a young girl
chosen queen and her court…
roundabout through the village
and into the church for mass.

A *festa* follows,
serving Sopas de Hortelã.
Everyone in the village
and beyond,
regardless of creed,
is invited.
No one shall ever go hungry
at Pentecost
from the moment after mass
when white doves are released
into the heavens.

In California
and other states
wherever Azorean descendants live,
the Holy Spirit is honored
in traditional
Feasts of Pentecost.

"Remember, Mother,
when we were in the island plane,"
says Maria,
"the first time I saw

Beef in Herbal
Broth

*Molha*
*Sopas de Hortelã*

page 160–1

the top of Pico shining in the sun
and the rest of it
we could not see in the mist…
I fumbled for my camera
and you said not to worry
that it would happen again?"
I remembered.
"At no time in the week
that we have been in Pico
has it happened again."

"Maria, I am sorry.
I should have known better."

She consoles me, adding,
"I've learned a lesson.
Certain things happen only once,
and I must act then
to freeze them forever
in that one instant in time."

Maria and her camera and I
walk around the village.
An elderly lady dressed in black
sees us,
walks over to converse.
She appears disappointed that
Maria cannot speak Portuguese.
She poses the inevitable question,
"Why is a pretty girl like you
not married?"

As I interpret the question,
Maria bristles, says to me,
"Tell her I have a boyfriend.
Tell her we live together."
"What does she say?"

the woman asks.
"Oh," I smile sweetly,
"She wants you to know
that she is betrothed."

We visit the last survivor
of his generation,
a cousin of my father's,
addressed as Uncle
by those of my generation
and their descendants.
Tio Inacio
and his wife Camelia
invite us to dinner at noon.

Diane and Maria leave earlier
with Fernando
to tour parts of the Island.
He will drop them off in time.

Because we are late arriving
at Tio Inacio's home,
Diane and Maria are there
looking bewildered,
trying to communicate.

Tio Inacio looks up
with his piercing blue eyes,
the bluest I have ever seen.
He greets us smiling.
After introductions and embraces,
he tells us, laughing,
"As I was dozing off,
I suddenly see two lovely girls.
'Surely this is a vision,'
I think to myself.
'I must be in heaven.'"

My daughters beam as I interpret
his welcome words.

Camelia guides us indoors,
sits us at a round table
set with pretty china, like Gloria's,
on an embroidered white cloth.
She serves traditional fish
in molho cru, an uncooked
sauce of crushed garlic
and parsley in wine,
seasoned with other herbs...
taro root called inhames,
greens related to cabbage,
and red Pico wine.

Taro Root

*Inhames*

*page 158*

So engaging is Tio Inacio's
conversation that one entirely
forgets that he sits
in a wheelchair
with, from the knee down,
one empty trouser leg.

Aurea and Jose Lourenco
invite the five of us with
Amaro, Fatima, and Marilia,
to her aunt's *adega*
for an evening dinner.

We hike down to the sea
and zig-zag back
through other walkways.

Seated at more than one table,
we enjoy the usual pork
and taro root and linguiça,
greens and red Pico wine.

Aurea serves a new dish
that we will long remember,
octopus, *polvo*, cooked
in a delicious herb sauce…
rice pudding for dessert.

As we sit in the courtyard
looking out and conversing
in the spring twilight,
I notice an *arv de nespras*,
a loquat tree.
The fruit appears to be ripe.
"Children, please get some,"
someone asks.

The children run down the hill
and swing over the orchard wall.
Rubene returns
with a large bowl filled
with one-inch-diameter
glossy balls of a deep yellow,
first fruit of the season.
Sea breezes have honed
both the flesh and the fragrance.
They taste even better than
those of my hilltop acre
in California.
"A delight for the soul," I say,
assembling all the brown seeds
into a glossy pile on my plate.

Our last evening in Santo Amaro,
all the cousins gather
for a dinner
at Amaro's *adega*.
A sense of goodbye
silently invades the atmosphere

Rice Pudding

*Arroz Doce*

*page 172*

as we chatter,
sitting closely
around the huge round table,
food illumined by candlelight.
No waning moon yet visible
in the dark of the night,
a *fogo*, a bonfire, burns
on the roadway
in front of the *adega*.

Holding hands in a circle,
we dance around the fire.
The children sing
some American pop songs
they memorized from recordings.
One of their favorites,
"I Just Called to Say I Love You."
The parents laugh, saying,
"That isn't really music."

Diane and Maria sing
songs from American musicals.
Everyone urges them to keep singing.
They oblige with several classics,
more operettas, ending with
"Give me your tired and your poor…"
and "The Impossible Dream."

Everyone sings
the songs they all know and love,
"Glory, Glory Hallelujah"
"Row, Row your boat…"
English and Portuguese words
blend with the tunes.
Music,
the universal language…
songs linger long in the memory.

Rapidly comes the morning
of our departure.
Maria films our rising-sun exit.
We kiss Marilia
before she leaves for school,
kiss Mara, now recuperating
but still restricted indoors.
A friend of her grandmother's
has come to stay with her.
Gloria, Fatima, and Amaro
take us to the *aeroporto.*

I wait,
conversing in weighted words,
hoping to leave nothing unsaid,
wonder when we will meet again,
laugh to conceal emotion.

Misty-eyed embraces,
promises to return some day,
*se Deus queser,*
God willing,
we board the island-hopping plane,
the one with the Rolls-Royce symbol,
to the *aeroporto* at Terceira.

I look down on Pico,
make the sign of the cross,
ask God to bless and keep
Our Island
and everyone on it.
*Saudades…Saudades…*

A full day is left of our vacation,
a day to tour
the Island of Terceira…
white sandy beaches,

white seafoam on black rocks,
grapevines over lava-rock walls,
pyramids of stacked corncobs,
exotic gardens,
wrought-iron balconies…
old monasteries
at peace with the years
on the island of monuments.

We identify with the brochures
as they point out
grey fortresses
that preserve memories
of ships from the Far East,
anchoring in sheltered coves and bays,
São Baptista Fortress by Monte Brasil,
bullfights
where the bull is never killed
in São Sebastião Ampitheater
from May to November.

We stay at Angra do Heroismo,
oldest town in the Islands,
founded in 1534.

We walk past
old cottages overgrown with vines,
wish there was a concert today
in the city park,
a forest of greens
punctuated with multicolored flowers,
inviting imaginary strollers,
poets and musicians,
inviting us
to stroll this day in May.

Back to Terceira Aeroporto
to wait for the plane
TAP Flight 316Y,
held up while our Airforce One
takes off with our President
on his return from Portugal
after negotiating renewal of
U.S. airbase rights
in the Azores Islands.

Airborne now,
eager to get home,
I look one last time
at the Island of Terceira
soon to exist for me
only in memory.

The long journey ahead
offers time
to think of our experiences,
to think about our cousins,
to do a preliminary summing-up.
It is too soon
to put it all together.
That will come much later.
In the meantime, our hosts
with whom we lived two weeks,
remain etched in my memory.

*Amaro*
no longer has the red beard
I had seen in a photograph
when he played a king
in local theatrics.
Perhaps his approaching forty
accounts for his thinning hair.
I gave him a solar calculator.

He knew of them, said
they had none in the village.
He will have uses for it,
especially to total the wages,
as a building crew foreman,
of those who work for him.

He told us of his four years
in the military in Angola.
He does not believe in colonialism,
feels Portugal should have granted
independence to its colonies
long before she did.
He feels fortunate
to have come home alive and well,
bearing tapestries and woolen
blankets from those foreign lands.

Farmer, winemaker, builder,
fisherman, thinker concerned
about the human condition,
member of the church choir...
He lives in rhythm with the sea
and with the growing seasons.

*Fatima*
of the merry almond-shaped eyes,
exudes a mysterious appeal.
Maker of palate-pleasing desserts,
she is much her own person,
active in church and community,
quick to speak out
on political issues
espoused by television politicians.
Though very much alive
to new ideas,
she and Amaro honor tradition

by living in the family home
with her mother.
As a balance, their family
often spends weekends alone
in their *adega.*

*Marilia*
petite older daughter
wishes she were taller.
An avid reader, she dislikes
some compulsory subjects.
Reads also very well in English
but is too timid to speak it,
faithfully performs the assigned task
of setting the traditional table
in the Continental fashion
with the dessert spoon-fork
horizontally placed
above the dinner plate,
left of the wine glass.

*Mara*
child of the sea
for which she is named.
One catches a glimpse in her
of the restlessness
of the ever-changing sea
and a longing
for faraway places.
Long-legged,
she leaps gracefully
from one stone to another
on her way to and from
the rocky shore.

Both children in their speech
display a sophistication

beyond their years.
Azoreans cater to no youth cult.

Both girls love sports,
complain the government
spends far more
on sports for the boys,
short-changing the girls.

*Gloria*
too young to qualify
as a matriarch…
rightly proclaimed
artist of embroideries,
crocheting, knitting, sewing.
She spends hours creating
clothes for the family,
often remodeling castaways
sent by cousins from the U.S.
Her savory sauces,
fish and meats, assembled
on platters, are worthy
of exhibition on magazine covers.
I remember watching her prepare
a panful of fish
Amaro had just caught.
She covered them with cut-up
onion, garlic, and other herbs,
pouring a half-bottle of wine
over them before baking.
She says she is fortunate
to live in the most beautiful
part of God's Earth.

*Arminda* and *Helio*
broke the tradition
of living together with parents

in one of the family homes.
Her parents,
Silverio and Maria,
presented the newlywed couple
with the lava-rock house
her father remodeled himself.
The house is not far
from their parents' home,
my mother's childhood home,
inherited by Silverio.
They also gave their daughter
a new compact car
to drive to work
in the office
of the local hospital.
She needed it, they say,
because the couple
works different hours.

During our stay
at no time did I miss
a telephone,
even forgot about it.
Villagers, on their daily rounds,
deliver messages for each other.

Not every family owns a car,
accounting for the unspoiled air.
A friend in another village
complained that the exhaust
from too many cars had already
destroyed the subtle fragrance
of certain trees and plants.
Yet, she herself drives a car.

In the arts, music excels.
Besides the church choir,

every village has a band
that plays in the church square
on a specially designed stage.
Bands are invited to perform
in each other's villages
on *festa* days.
People of all ages make up
the choir and the band.
Occasionally, villagers
perform in the theater
in dramas and musicals.

Aspiring painters eventually
head for the mainland.
A wood carver carves at home.
A relative of Tio Inacio
writes poetry.

Intent on preserving
the ancient arts,
the government dispenses funds
for summer vacation classes.
Girls in old-fashioned
embroidered gowns and caps
sit embroidering
alongside wood carvers,
lacemakers, knitters,
wool and straw weavers,
painters, potterers, sketchers...
to each his own.

Only the school has a library.
The nearest bookstore
in Madalena also sells
an assortment of magazines.
I recognize *Time*
and *Reader's Digest,*

both in Portuguese.
A weekly newspaper
comes from Faial
as do the television programs.


As I relive
the fleeting interlude
in our lives,
I wonder if I will ever return,
or if in the rush
of daily living
I will want to return
to the Island of my ancestors,
now Our Island.
This visit was almost too perfect,
one that seems preordained.
Is it better to leave it that way?
I wonder.

Ed and I often talked
of coming here together,
not knowing then it was not to be.
Yet, spiritually,
he has been with me
all the way.

We arrive at Kennedy Airport
in late afternoon,
go through customs,
waiting impatiently in line,
too late to connect
with United Flight 1650,
a direct flight to Sacramento.

TAP finds us hotel rooms in New York.
I fall asleep in the middle
of "MacNeil/Lehrer NewsHour."
We sleep off our jet lag,
board another United flight
the next morning
by way of Denver
to Sacramento.

At the end of our journey
all our families
welcome us at the airport,
embracing us with happy chatter
just like the multitude
of cousins
who welcomed us
on the Atlantic shore.
We five agree
it is good to know
love follows us
wherever we go
to and from
the Atlantic and the Pacific.

Every journey
involves some kind of search,
sometimes for we know not what.
For what was I searching?
I did not know.
Have I found it?
I certainly have.

Since that time
wherever I wander
wherever I go,
echoes of memories
keep following me,
echoes of familiar sounds,
echoes of haunting melodies…
*Saudades…Saudades…*

Songs of Saudades…

*Azorean American Recipes*

Cooking is an art.
Consider the aroma and eye-appeal
of golden brown freshly baked bread,
a green soup,
fish in molha cru,
the tomatoes and onion
and various greens in a salad,
rainbow tidbits of dried fruits and nuts
in a Christmas fruitcake.

Any tantalizing, tasty, palate-pleasing
dish cooked with imagination
and served with love
involves all the senses,
even a sixth sense,
and becomes truly a work of art.
It is to be contemplated
and viewed in the same way
that one enjoys a poem,
a painting,
a ballet,
a musical composition.

All enrich the enjoyable life
that the Good Lord wants for us
in our sojourn on Planet Earth.
All lead to the ultimate universal
Art of Living.

# *Holidays for special foods . . .*

| | |
|---|---|
| Páscoa | Easter |
| Espírito Santo | Pentecost |
| Natal | Christmas |
| Dia de Ano Novo | New Year's Day |

| | |
|---|---|
| Aguardente | Brandy |
| Angelica | Sweet dessert wine often poured over fruit as in a fruit cup |
| Red Pico wine | Dinner wine |

# BREAD

## Unleavened Cake-Bread
### *Bolo do Forno*

3    cups white Corn Flour
1    teaspoon Salt
7    cups boiling Water
$2^2/_3$    cups white Flour
2    tablespoons Sugar

Pour boiling water over corn flour
and salt, and stir until smooth.
As it hardens and cools,
add white flour and sugar
and knead thoroughly
until polished-looking.
Divide dough into three balls,
flatten each one like a pancake
about one-half-inch thick
and bake in a pre-heated
450-degree F. oven
until golden brown,
about one hour.
Place on a wire rack to cool.

*Bolo, an unleavened cake-bread,*
*is a Portuguese quick bread*
*like the baking powder biscuits*
*of our pioneer days.*

# Whole Wheat Bread
## *Pão de Trigo*

| | |
|---|---|
| 5 | cups regular Flour |
| 2 | cups whole wheat Flour |
| 4 | pkgs rapid-rise dry Yeast |
| 2 | teaspoons Salt |
| 3 | tablespoons Sugar |
| 2 | cups Water |
| ½ | cup Milk |
| 2 | tablespoons Margarine |

In a bowl combine 2½ cups
of the mixed measured flours.
Add sugar, salt and yeast.
Heat water, milk and margarine
from 120 to 130 degrees F.
A candy thermometer
will omit the need for guessing.
Gradually add the heated milk-
water-margarine mixture to dry
mixture in the kneading bowl.
Beat with electric mixer at medium
speed about two minutes, add
½ cup more of the flour and beat
on high for two more minutes.
Add enough of the measured flour
to make a soft dough.

Knead until smooth and elastic
until it no longer sticks to your hands.
Cover dough and let rest ten minutes.
Shape dough into loaves,
cover and let rise in warm place
until double in bulk,
about sixty to ninety minutes.
Do finger test…
if impression remains,
the dough is through rising.
Bake in preheated 400-degree F. oven
until done…
an attractive golden brown…
thirty minutes or more.
Remove loaves from pans
and set on wire racks to cool.

# Sweet Bread
## *Pão Doce*

*These are single-crusted sweet rolls,
baked without touching each other
to achieve a lot of crustiness.
If served for Easter,
it is called Pão de Páscoa...
for Pentecost,
Pão de Espírto Santo,
Holy Spirit Bread...
for Christmas,
Pão de Natal.
In our family,
we called them Biscoitos.*

| | |
|---|---|
| 7 | cups regular Flour |
| 1½ | cups Sugar |
| ½ | teaspoon Salt |
| 4 | pkgs rapid-rise dry Yeast |
| 1 | cup Milk |
| ¼ | cup Water |
| ¼ | cup Margarine or Butter |
| 6 | Eggs |

In a large bowl, place two cups
of the measured flour.
Add sugar and salt
and undissolved dry yeast.
In a smaller bowl, beat eggs...add
¾ cup of the flour and continue
beating until smooth...set aside.
Heat milk-water-margarine mixture
from 120 to 130 degrees F.
and add to dry ingredients
in large kneading bowl.
Beat at high speed two minutes.
Add beaten-egg mixture...
continue beating until smooth.
Add remainder of measured flour.
Knead by hand until smooth
and elastic and until it no longer
sticks to your hands.
If necessary, when kneading,
add a little more flour,
not too much.
Cover and let stand ten minutes.
Mold and shape as desired,
place on slightly greased pans,
not touching each other...
put in warm place to rise
until double in bulk.
Do finger test...if impression remains,
the dough is through rising.
Bake in pre-heated 350-degree F.
oven....15 to 17 minutes for small
rolls, about four inches in diameter.
When golden brown,
remove from oven and rub
with margarine or butter until glossy.
Set rolls on wire racks to cool.
This recipe can easily
be doubled and even tripled.

# CULINARY GLOSSARY

Bouquet of Herbs
  Pickling Spice tied in a
  cloth bag to cook in meat
  broth and afterwards
  discarded.

Garlic Salt
  Sometimes added to enhance
  the taste of garlic already
  included in dish.

Hortelã
  Garden mint.

Inhames
  Taro Root…the same root the
  Hawaiians let ferment and
  call poi. It is also the root
  of the ornamental plant
  known as Elephant Ears.

Linguiça
  A sausage made of pork loin,
  marinated in Vinho-de-Alhos.

Pickling Spice
  Contains mustard seed,
  coriander, bay leaves,
  ginger, chiles, cloves,
  cinnamon, allspice, mace,
  cardamom, black pepper.

Poultry Seasoning
  Contains thyme, sage,
  marjoram, rosemary,
  black pepper, nutmeg.

Seafood Seasoning
  Contains salt, celery
  seed, mustard, thyme,
  ginger, peppers,
  allspice, bay leaves.

Sopas
  Partly stale bread saturated with
  meat broth…saturated but not
  soaked…eaten with the meat
  whence came the broth.

Sopas de Leite
  Bread saturated in cold
  milk…a favorite quick,
  satisfying meal for
  a tired child or adult.

Torta
  A small round cake made by
  frying cut-up meat or fish
  mixtures blended
  with beaten eggs and dropped by
  spoonfuls on hot oil or margarine
  in a skillet, each turned over once
  and fried slowly until done.

Vinho-de-Alhos
  Marinade for pork made
  with wine vinegar and
  garlic.

# *SOUP*

## Green Soup
### *Caldo Verde*

In a soup kettle, saute in olive oil
a couple of cut-up onions,
some cut-up stalks of celery,
and a couple of cut-up garlic cloves.
Add several cut-up garden tomatoes
or a can of peeled tomatoes
and two or three stems of parsley.
Add the greens of choice, coarsely
cut-up turnip greens, chard, kale,
collard, or any other favorite green.
Add beef or chicken stock
or bouillon beef or chicken powder
dissolved in ½ cup boiling water,
enough stock to flavor eight or so
cups of water at the ratio of one
teaspoon to a cup of water.
Add a cup of brown rice.
Add a blend of your favorite herbs,
salt and pepper, and garlic powder.
Bring soup to a rolling boil.
Turn down heat to simmering…
simmer for about an hour.
If you like, add a cup or so
of canned kidney beans
or a can of vegetarian refried
beans about 15 minutes
before the soup is done…
a hearty satisfying meal.

# FISH AND MEAT

## Fish in Uncooked Sauce
### *Peixe em Molho Cru*

Place fish that has been fried or baked
on a platter and pour Molho Cru over
it before serving.

## *Molho Cru*

In a mortar (*gral*), combine six cut-up
cloves of garlic, a pinch of salt,
and a handful of cut-up parsley.
Crush into a mixture and add enough
vinegar to form a paste and more
to wash out the mortar after mixture
is transferred to a bowl.
Add water slowly, tasting to acquire
the degree of tanginess desired.

*Good served with boiled potatoes,
boiled or baked sweet potatoes,
or boiled taro root.
Serve with a vegetable
and a salad with mayonnaise-type
dressing. Do not use oil and
vinegar dressing as it will compete
with the taste of the Molho Cru.*

# Fish in Tomato Sauce
## *Peixe em Molho de Tomate*

| | |
|---|---|
| 6 | Fish Fillets or Steaks |
| 1 | yellow Onion |
| 6 | green Onions |
| ½ | pound Mushrooms |
| 1 | 16 oz. can Tomatoes or fresh tomatoes |

In a large kettle, saute in olive oil
cut-up yellow and green onions,
a few stalks of cut-up celery,
and several cut-up mushrooms.
Add a 16-ounce can of peeled
tomatoes or the equivalent of
fresh tomatoes from your garden
that have been peeled and cut up.
Add a pinch of fish seasoning,
garlic powder, salt and pepper.
Simmer about one-half hour.
Add washed fish slices or fillets
and simmer about 20 to 30
minutes or less,…that is
until fish becomes flaky
when tested with a fork…
do not overcook.

*Serve with boiled potatoes,*
*boiled or baked sweet potatoes,*
*or boiled taro root.*

# Taro Root
## *Inhames*

Arrange washed taros in a large
kettle and add enough cold water
to cover them.
Adjust kettle lid to fit tightly.
Bring water to a rolling boil
and turn heat down to simmering.
Simmer for seven hours
for the very large ones,
five hours for the medium ones,
and three hours for the small ones.
If water simmers down,
add more water to cover taros.
Add about three tablespoons of salt
at the last hour of cooking
and finish simmering.

Remove taros from kettle
to a platter to cool.
When cold, refrigerate for later
use within a week.
Do not cover in refrigerator as
they tend to become mushy.
Taros may also be frozen
for serving at a later time.
Freeze in a paper wrapping.
Plastic wrap tends to make them
somewhat mushy as they thaw.

To heat, slice lengthwise and
fry slowly in oil or margarine
until a crisp coating develops.
Bacon or roasted pork drippings,
and even linguiça drippings,
were the previous choices
and were delicious,
but no longer chosen
for health reasons.

Good served with pork, ham,
bacon, linguiça, fish, or eggs.

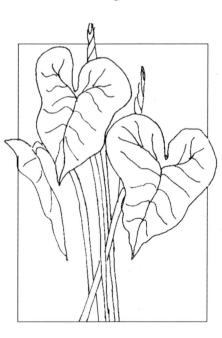

# Aunt Mimi's Tuna Tortas

*In memory of my Aunt Amelia*
*who was more like a sister to me.*

In a bowl, combine a six-ounce can
of tuna…packed in water, not oil.
Add cut-up green onions,
a cut-up handful of parsley.
a sprinkle of garlic powder,
a sprinkle of fish seasoning,
and a pinch of salt.
Add six beaten eggs
and mix thoroughly.
Into a large skillet,
with hot olive oil or margarine,
drop mixture by spoonful
to make individual small tortas.
When bubbly, turn each over
to finish cooking.
Arrange on a platter to serve.
Leftovers heated,
make good-tasting sandwiches
with mayonnaise, mustard,
and lettuce or cabbage leaves.

# Beef in Herbal Broth
## *Molha*

6–8  pound Chuck Roast
1  medium Onion, cut up
2  stalks Celery, cut up
2  8-ounce cans Tomato Sauce
3  tablespoons Red Wine Vinegar
Bouquet of Pickling Spice

Place roast in large kettle and
add water and tomato sauce to
cover. Add onion and celery
and red wine vinegar.
Bring to a rolling boil.
Toss in the bouquet made by
enclosing in cloth the pickling
spices and tying it with thread.
Cover kettle and turn heat lower.
Simmer two or three hours
until meat is done.
Skim off fat before serving.
Taste broth…if more tanginess
is desired, add more vinegar.

Serve with boiled white potatoes
or boiled or baked sweet potatoes.
This is the traditional dish served
after Midnight Mass on Christmas.

*Served with Sopas de Hortelã,
it becomes the traditional dish
served for Pentecost, and is then
called Sopas de Espírito Santo.*

# Sopas de Hortelã

Arrange slices of partly stale crusty
bread in a large, deep serving dish.
Cover with two or three sprigs of
garden mint and with a little boiling
hot Molha broth. Repeat,
adding two or three layers,
ending with mint on top.
Add just enough broth
so it saturates the layers of bread.
Do not soak the sopas…extra broth
can be served in a bowl
to pass around at the table.
Cover the dish of sopas and place
in a warm oven about ten minutes
before serving.
Cut the roast into serving pieces,
place on a platter, and top with
sprigs of garden mint and spoon
a little broth over it…place platter
in warm oven with sopa dish
to rest ten minutes before serving.

*At Pentecost, my mother served
with the Sopas de Espírito Santo
a side dish of our tasty American
potato salad…a good combination.*

# Pork in Wine and Garlic
## *Torresmos*

Cut up a pork roast into rectangles
approximately three by five inches,
or two by four inches.
Place them in a large pan of glass,
 stoneware, stainless steel
or use a crock-type of container,
to be marinated.
Do not use a vessel
made of aluminum.

## *Vinho-de-Alhos Marinade*

In a bowl, crush 10 to 12 cloves
of garlic in a couple teaspoons of salt.
Add the juice of two lemons
and one cup of Red Wine Vinegar.
Dilute with enough water to attain
the desired tang…adding more
vinegar if necessary.
Cut up and toss in the lemon rind.
Pour the marinade over the meat.
The marinade should inundate
the rectangles of pork.
Cover and refrigerate overnight.
To roast, remove the meat
from the marinade,
drain and place in a baking pan…
not aluminum…

Throw away the marinade.
Bake about two hours
in a 350-degree F. oven
until well done and browned.
Drain off any fat
that accumulated.
Serve with baked or boiled white
or sweet potatoes or taro root.
Serve one or two vegetables
in the cabbage family.
If serving a salad,
use a mayonnaise-type dressing.
Do not use an oil and vinegar
dressing, which would compete
with the taste
of the Vinho-de-Alhos.

# Pork Roast and Stuffing
## *Carne de Porco Assada e Debulho*

Purchase a half leg of pork
and ask the butcher to remove
the bone and tie up the meat.
He will give you the removed bone.
You can freeze it to cook with beans
sometime later on.
Also ask him for a few strips of fat.
At the same time, purchase a pound
of pork sausage for the stuffing.

When preparing the meat
for roasting,
trim off and save any fat
visible to the eye and set aside.
Peel and cut into slivers
a few cloves of garlic
and insert into cuts here and there
along the leg of pork.

Rub a little red wine vinegar all
over the roast and sprinkle with
garlic powder, salt and pepper.
Whatever pieces of fat
you salvaged and purchased,
cut in strips or pieces and place
on top and sides of the roast
and anchor each with a toothpick.
Roast in a 350-degree F. oven
for four, five, or six hours,
depending on actual poundage,

at 35 to 40 minutes per pound,
until well done.
A meat thermometer can be
inserted at thickest part of the meat.
It will tell you when the roast is done
at 180 degrees F.
Slip into the oven
a large casserole full of stuffing
to bake the last two hours
along with the pork roast.

*When my mother came*
*to my father's homestead in Idaho*
*as a young bride*
*from the Azores Islands,*
*I am told she served the traditional*
*Molha for Christmas dinner.*
*Later she adopted the traditional*
*American turkey and stuffing*
*which I remember and followed*
*when it came my turn to cook*
*the Christmas dinner.*
*Because my grandson Jim*
*is allergic to all fowl,*
*I decided several years ago*
*to serve a roast leg of pork*
*rubbed with red wine vinegar*
*and served with a special stuffing.*
*My family was delighted*
*and insisted this be our traditional*
*family Christmas dinner.*

# Stuffing for Pork Roast
## *Debulho*

| | | | |
|---|---|---|---|
| 1 | loaf sliced whole wheat Bread | 3 | large yellow Onions |
| 2 | loaves crusty white Bread | 3 | green Onions |
| 1 | pound Pork Sausage | 8 | oz. carton of Mushrooms |
| 1 | bunch of Celery | 1 | bunch of Parsley |
| | | 8 | Chicken Bouillon cubes |

A week before, purchase the bread.
Pierce the wrappings to stale.
When ready to make the stuffing,
cut the stale bread into cubes,
mixing the whole wheat and white.
Put into a large pan and set aside.

In a large kettle, fry the sausage
until well done.
Remove sausage and set aside.
Saute in the same kettle
after discarding most of the fat
the cut-up outer celery stalks,
the yellow and green onions,
mushrooms and 3 stalks parsley,
no parsley leaves at this point.
When properly sauted,
stir in the cooked sausage.
and let stand with heat off.

Cut up a whole bunch of parsley
leaves and add to cubed breads.
Heat in microwave a cup of water
to which has been added eight
chicken bouillon cubes.

When dissolved, pour bouillon
liquid into a quart and a half
of cold tap water and set aside.

Mix parsley leaves and breads,
adding about three teaspoons
poultry seasoning, and a heavy
sprinkle of garlic powder.
Add onion-sausage mixture
to bread crumbs...mix thoroughly.
Add one quart of bouillon water
and mix well...slowly adding more
bouillon liquid as necessary...
not too much....not too little.
Mix until easy to handle...
not too wet...not too dry.
Break in two raw eggs and mix
thoroughly to right consistency.
Pack into a large greased casserole
or more than one casserole dish.
Rub a little margarine over top.
Bake at least two hours
in a 350-degree F. oven during
the last two hours the pork bakes
so they finish together.

# Gravy

When pork is done, remove
from roasting pan and keep hot.
Discard all fat from pan and
pour hot water into pan to salvage
the brown for the gravy.
Pour eight cups of water,
into which has been dissolved
eight bouillon cubes,
and bring to a boil…
add poultry seasoning and pepper
and salt and garlic powder to taste.
Thicken with flour and water
shaken in a large jar.
Ratio is two tablespoons flour
to one cup of water.
Bring to a boil and simmer.

*Cranberry sauce and Applesauce*
*are both good with the roast pork.*
*Serve with mashed potatoes and/or*
*sweet potatoes, a vegetable or two,*
*and your favorite salad…red dinner*
*wine, champagne, or sparkling cider,*
*and a Christmas dessert…*
*and enjoy a Merry Christmas dinner.*

# DESSERTS

## Mama's Carrot Cake
### *Bolo de Cenoura*

*This cake is in memory of my mother,
Marian Ineas.
It is a revision of the carrot pudding
she baked in the pressure cooker.
It looked like a round cake...
served warm with whipped cream.
My revision is baked in the oven
and tastes the same as her pudding.*

¾   cup Margarine
⅓   cup Sugar
1½  cups dark Molasses
4   Eggs
¾   cup Orange Juice
    grated Orange Rind
3   cups regular Flour
1   cup whole wheat Flour
3   teaspoons Baking Soda
1½  teaspoons Cinnamon
½   teaspoon Salt
3   cups shredded Carrots
1   cup chopped Walnuts
1   cup Raisins

In a large bowl
mix margarine and molasses.
Add eggs and beat until smooth.
Add orange juice, mix well.
Add flour-soda-cinnamon-salt
mixture...mix thoroughly.
Stir in carrots and walnuts.
Baked in a greased sheetcake pan,
or two bundt pans
or two loaf pans

or a combination of pans
35 to 45 minutes
in a 350-degree F. oven until done.
Cool in the pan on a wire rack.

This moist cake needs no icing.
Sprinkle powdered sugar on each
serving at the time of serving...
or top with a spoon of vanilla
ice cream or orange sherbet.

# Orange-Date Pinwheels
## *Bolachas de Laranja e Tamareiras*

**Date Filling**
Make a date filling…
combining one cup chopped dates,
¼ cup orange juice,
¼ cup sugar
and some orange rind.
Simmer, stirring until thick.
Cool…add ½ cup cut-up walnuts.
Set aside.

*Orange-Date Pinwheels are only one among the many variations of Ice Box Cookies baked in the days before gas and electric refrigerators and freezers became available.*

**Cookie Dough**

| | | | | |
|---|---|---|---|---|
| ½ | cup Margarine | | 1 | tablespoon Lemon Juice |
| 1 | cup Sugar | | 3 | cups regular Flour |
| 1 | Egg | | ½ | teaspoon Baking Soda |
| | grated Orange Rind | | ½ | teaspoon Salt |
| 3 | teaspoons Orange Juice | | | |

Mix margarine and sugar.
Add egg and beat.
Add orange and lemon juice
and orange rind
and beat until smooth.
Add flour-soda-salt mixture
and mix thoroughly.
Divide dough into three parts.
On three sheets of wax paper,
roll each part into a rectangle.
Place on each
one-third of the date mixture
and spread evenly over the dough.
Roll each rectangle,
keeping it in the wax paper,

into a sealed-at-the-ends roll.
Refrigerate and freeze…
recipe can be easily doubled.

When ready to bake,
preheat oven to 350 degrees F.
Cut frozen rolls
with a sharp knife
into thin rounds
and place on cookie sheets.
Bake ten to twelve minutes
until light golden brown.
Cool on a wire rack.
Store in shallow cookie cans
standing on edge in one layer.

*My husband's mother,*
*Amelia Nunes,*
*made the best fruitcake*
*I have ever tasted.*
*Also well remembered*
*is her Kiss-Me-Cake.*
*I offer these in her memory.*

# Nana's Fruitcake
## *Bolo de Fruta Passada*

| | |
|---|---|
| 6 | cups Raisins |
| 2 | cups Dates, cut-up |
| 1 | cup dried Figs, cut-up |
| 1 | cup dried Apricots, cut-up |
| 1 | cup Corn Syrup |
| ½ | cup Sherry Wine or Angelica |
| 1 | pound mixed Glazed Fruits containing citron, cherries, pineapple, citrus peels Glazed Cherries for decorating |

In a covered dish or pan…
not aluminum…
stainless steel works well,
mix fruit in syrup and wine,
and let soak overnight.
Cover tightly to prolong aroma.
Mix the cake part the next day,
after lining the baking pans
with greased wax paper
over a layer of greased brown paper.

1½  cups Margarine
3   cups Brown Sugar
8   Eggs
4   cups regular Flour
1½  teaspoons Baking Soda
½   teaspoon Salt
2   teaspoons Cinnamon
½   teaspoon Cloves
1½  teaspoons Nutmeg
½   cup Orange Juice
4   cups Walnuts, chopped…
    if desired, mix with
    chopped Almonds or Pecans

Cream margarine and sugar.
Add eggs gradually, beating well.
Add flour-soda-salt-spice mixture.
Mix well and add to soaked fruit.
Blend throughly with orange juice.
If mixture appears too moist,
add about a cup of flour.
Bake the ten-pound fruitcake
in five loaves
or two rings and one loaf
or three loaves and one ring.
Decorate with walnuts and cherries
on top of each cake before baking.
Bake two and a half hours

in a 275-degree F. oven
with the rack in the middle
of the oven
and a pan of boiling water
on the oven floor for steaming.
When done, cool on wire racks.

Store in tightly covered containers
with a quarter apple in each can,
replacing when apple dries out.
Bake cakes in October
for Thanksgiving Day
and in November
for Christmas and the New Year.

# Nana's Kiss-Me Cake
## *Bolo de Beijar-Me*

1    large Orange
1    tablespoon Lemon Juice

Squeeze the orange,
add lemon juice to orange juice
to equal one-third cup,
and reserve juice
to pour over cake after baking.
Grind or cut up finely
orange pulp and rind
and set aside.

½    cup Margarine
1⅓    cups Sugar
4    Eggs
1    cup Milk
3    cups regular Flour

1    cup whole wheat Flour
2    teaspoons Baking Soda
½    teaspoon Salt
1    cup Raisins
1    cup Walnuts, chopped

Cream margarine and sugar.
Add eggs and beat thoroughly.
Add orange pulp and mix well.
Stir in milk
and flour-soda-salt mixture.
Add raisin and walnuts
and blend thoroughly.
Bake in a greased sheet-cake pan
in a 350-degree F. oven
from forty to fifty minutes.

When done, remove from oven,
prick all over gently with toothpick,
and pour reserved
strained orange-lemon juice
very slowly over hot cake.
Cool in the pan on a rack.
Serve with a cinnamon-sugar
sprinkles…whipped cream…
or a spoon of vanilla ice cream…
or a spoon of orange sherbet.

# Gingerbread Cookies
## *Bolachas de Pão de Gengibre*

|   |   |
|---|---|
| 4 | cups old-fashioned Oats |
| 2½ | cups hot Water |
| 1 | cup Raisins |

In a large mixing bowl,
pour two cups hot water over oats.
Stir in raisins and let stand to cool,
reserving one-half cup water for later.

|   |   |   |   |
|---|---|---|---|
| 1 | cup Margarine | ½ | teaspoon Salt |
| 1 | cup Sugar | 1½ | teaspoons Ginger |
| 5 | Eggs | 1½ | teaspoons Cinnamon |
| 1 | 12-oz. bottle dark Molasses | ½ | teaspoon Allspice |
| 7½ | cups Flour | 1 | cup chopped Walnuts |
| 1½ | teaspoons Baking Soda |   |   |

In another bowl,
cream margarine and sugar
until smooth.
Add eggs and beat thoroughly.
Stir in molasses, using the reserved
one-half cup of water
to rinse out the bottle…
add rinsed water and mix well.
Add mixture to oats
and mix thoroughly.
Add the flour-soda-salt-spice
mixture and walnuts.
Finish mixing by wooden spoon
to achieve a stiff dough.
Add more flour or water if needed.

Cover bowl with wax paper
and chill in the refrigerator
a couple of hours
or, preferably, overnight.
If desired, a portion of the batter
can be frozen to bake later on.
To bake, place spoonfuls of batter
on ungreased baking sheet…
mold or leave each at random.
Bake in 375-degree F.
preheated oven
16 minutes more or less.
Cool on wire racks.
Yield is about one hundred cookies…
especially good for breakfast.

# Rice Pudding
## *Arroz Doce*

3   cups cooked brown Rice
½   cup Raisins
½   teaspoon Cinnamon
3   Eggs
2   cups Milk

In a glass loaf or casserole dish
place three cups cooked brown rice.
Mix in a heavy sprinkling of cinnamon
and a half cup of raisins.
In a bowl, beat slightly three eggs…
add two cups of dairy milk
or soy milk.
Mix milk and eggs
and pour over the rice mixture,
stirring and mixing thoroughly.
Bake in a 325-degree F. oven
about an hour until done
when an inserted dinner knife
comes out clean.
Cool on a wire rack and refrigerate.

*T*hese recipes represent
my family's adaptation
of Azorean cookery
to our taste.
They may differ here and there
from the original.
Most important,
each recipe possesses
memory-evoking powers
that become more and more vivid
with the passing years.
This collection poses
a challenge to future generations
to adapt its contents
to the taste of its family members.
Blessed with bountiful harvests
from this blessed land,
I would like to see
sitting with me
at life's banquet table
all my fellow Eartheans
to partake
of Earth's abundance
em amor e saudades…
in love and saudades.

# INDEX

# *ABOUT THE AUTHOR*

A native of Southern Idaho, Florence Ineas Nunes is the
oldest of nine daughters and the matriarch of the first American-born
generation in her family. She strives to preserve the old Azorean-
Portuguese traditions of her parents. She has been writing poetry and
prose for more than four decades and is a member of Wordsmith and
Range of Light in Auburn, and the Renaissance Society writers and
Chaparral Poets in Sacramento. A lover of nature, a philosopher and an
avid reader, Nunes is an activist in matters of peace, human rights and
social justice. She is greatly concerned with healing the planet and
identifies herself as an American Earthean.

# TZEDAKAH PUBLICATIONS

For additional copies of *Songs of Saudades,*
please send your name, address, daytime phone number,
and a check or money order payable to:

> Tzedakah Publications
> P.O. Box 221097
> Sacramento, CA 95822
> **916-452-1824** or **1-800-316-1824**

Each book is $12.95 plus tax & shipping. For quantity
discounts, call (916) 452-1824 or 1-800-316-1824.

**Sales tax:**
Please add 7.75% for books shipped to California
addresses.

**Shipping:**
$2 for shipping via U.S. mail, or
$4 for United Parcel Service,
plus 75¢ for each additional book.
Allow 3 weeks for U.S. mail and 10 days for UPS.

**Visa/Mastercard:**
You may order by mail or call (916) 452-1824 or
1-800-316-1824. Please be ready with the card number,
name on the card and expiration date.

**Fund-raising:**
*Songs of Saudades* is available to groups for fund-raising.
Please call (916) 452-1824 or 1-800-316-1824 for details.

Your satisfaction guaranteed or your money promptly refunded.